KU-700-663

OF NIGHT

RIVER OF OCEAN

THE WORLD
according to
HOMER
B·C·1000

THE ODYSSEY OF HOMER

The
Odyssey of Homer

RETOLD BY

Barbara Leonie Picard

ILLUSTRATED BY

Joan Kiddell-Monroe

London

OXFORD UNIVERSITY
PRESS

Oxford University Press, Ely House, London W. 1
GLASGOW NEW YORK TORONTO MELBOURNE WELLINGTON
CAPE TOWN SALISBURY IBADAN NAIROBI DAR ES SALAAM LUSAKA ADDIS ABABA
BOMBAY CALCUTTA MADRAS KARACHI LAHORE DACCA
KUALA LUMPUR SINGAPORE HONG KONG TOKYO

ISBN 0 19 274508 5

First published 1952
Reprinted 1960, 1962, 1965, 1967, 1971

PRINTED IN GREAT BRITAIN

PREFACE

SOMEWHERE around three thousand years ago, Homer wrote his great epic poem *The Odyssey* in which he told of the adventures and wanderings of Odysseus, one of the Greek heroes. Since that time, the poem has been translated from the Greek dialect in which it was written, or the story retold in another writer's words, countless times. Every boy and girl knows at least one of the adventures of Odysseus; how he heard the Sirens sing, perhaps, or how he outwitted the Cyclops, Polyphemus; and there have been published numerous volumes of stories for children taken from *The Odyssey*. But there does not seem to have been a complete retelling of the entire story of the poem for young people.

The story is so good that it seems a pity that boys and girls should not read the whole of it; and what I have tried to do in this book is to give the whole tale of *The Odyssey* as the exciting and wonderful adventure that it was.

None of the characters in *The Odyssey* was created by Homer. They are all either legendary figures and great heroes well known to the people of his day, or they are the gods and goddesses of the Greeks.

The Greeks did not believe in one god, but in several, each with his or her own particular attributes. To the Greeks, the sky, the sea, and the earth were divided up between the three divine brothers, Zeus, Poseidon, and Hades. Zeus, the father of gods and men, and the most important of all the Greek deities, ruled over the earth and the sky; Poseidon was lord of the seas and rivers, while

Hades was the god of all that is found under the earth and the guardian of the spirits of the dead. Hera, the wife of Zeus, was the queen of the gods; and the other chief deities were Apollo, the god of art and learning and all the daylight things of the world; his sister, Artemis the huntress, who was goddess of the chase and all wild creatures; Aphrodite, goddess of love and beauty; Athene, goddess of wisdom, who presided over all craft and skilfulness, whether of the hands or the mind; Ares, the god of war; and Hermes, who was their messenger. In the north of Greece is a mountain called Mount Olympus, and here, on the very summit of the peak, the Greeks believed the gods lived, in everlasting peace and joy.

But there was one occasion on which their peace was broken for a while, when the three goddesses, Hera, Aphrodite, and Athene, quarrelled among themselves as to which of them was the most beautiful. The gods could not decide for them, so they went down to earth, and in the land of Troy they found Paris, the young son of the king of that country, and asked him to say which of the three he considered the loveliest. He chose Aphrodite, and as a reward, she promised him the most beautiful woman in the world for his wife. Unfortunately, the most beautiful woman in the world was the Grecian, Helen, and she was already the wife of Menelaus, the king of Sparta. But Aphrodite kept her promise, and when, later, Paris was travelling through Greece, he became a guest in the house of Menelaus, and there Helen saw him and fell in love with him. When he returned home to Troy she went with him. Menelaus appealed to his brother Agamemnon, the greatest of all the kings in Greece, to help him recover his wife; and

Agamemnon called together all the leaders of the Greeks and with a mighty fleet they sailed for the Trojan coast, and laid siege to the city of Troy. The siege lasted for ten years, and at the end of that time the city fell. Most of the Trojan leaders were killed, and Menelaus won back Helen.

When the war was over, the Greeks set sail for their homes, and among them was Odysseus, the king of Ithaca, and it is the story of his eventful voyage that Homer tells in *The Odyssey*.

Barbara Leonie Picard

CONTENTS

Contents

PART III

Odysseus in Ithaca

PART ONE

Odysseus sails for Ithaca

I

Polyphemus the Cyclops

AFTER their ten-year-long war with the men of Troy was ended and the Trojan city had fallen in flames and smoke, the victorious Greeks gathered together their booty and their prisoners; and when the great King Agamemnon, who was in charge of all the Grecian host, had given the word, one by one all those leaders of the Greeks who had survived the fighting boarded their ships and set sail for home.

Among them was Odysseus, king of the little island of Ithaca, lying off the mainland of Greece. He and his men put out to sea in twelve ships of fifty oars, their white sails unfurled and their blue-painted prows thrusting through the waves as the wind filled the sails: nigh on sixty men on board each ship. And the heart of every man was happy as he thought how at last, after ten weary years of battle, he would once again see Ithaca, which was his home.

After a few days at sea, Odysseus and his men landed in the country of the Cicones, and because for ten years their minds had been filled with thoughts of war and strife, it did not seem to them an evil thing to fall unprovoked upon the Cicones in their coastland city, killing the men and driving off their cattle.

On the beach they divided the spoils so that each man in the twelve ships had an equal share; and when this was done, Odysseus urged that they should set sail at once. But they were arrogant in their success, and gave no heed to his advice; instead they built fires upon the shore and roasted meat and broke open the Cicones' wine-jars. And feasting their victory with looted food and drink all night, they gave no thought to the people whose city they had that day despoiled.

But the Cicones sent for help to others of their race, finer warriors than themselves, who lived inland and fought from chariots; and in the first light of dawn they swept down upon the Greeks as they camped on the shore. All the morning, fighting with their backs to the sea, the men of Odysseus held their own, but in the hours after midday they were overwhelmed by the Cicones and, fleeing to the ships, they put out to sea leaving the Cicones masters of the day. And when their numbers were counted Odysseus found that he had lost six men out of every ship.

Not many days later, the ships ran into a strong north wind which blew them from their course, and after nine days' sailing in the wrong direction the land of the Lotus-eaters came in sight. They put in to shore, and Odysseus, ever curious as to the customs of other lands, sent out three men to discover what manner of people dwelt in this country.

They found them a peaceable and lazy folk, who desired nothing more in life than to eat of the fruit of the lotus plant and dream away their time. The Lotus-eaters received the Greeks kindly, as was their way with strangers, and gave them lotus fruits to eat. Immediately they had tasted of this food, Odysseus' men lost all wish to return to their comrades on the shore and toil once more upon the waves on their voyage to Ithaca. Indeed, they cared no longer for their homes and wished only to remain in the country of the Lotus-eaters, idly eating the lotus fruits and dreaming the days away.

When they did not return to him, Odysseus went with others of his men to find what had befallen them. 'Perchance they may have met with savage folk who hold them prisoner, or perchance they may be slain,' he said. 'We may yet be in time to save them, or we may avenge their deaths.'

But he found his men sitting with the Lotus-eaters in quiet content, with no wish in the world but to remain there evermore. Odysseus and his followers dragged the three men back to the ships, protesting and wailing, and bound them firmly, lest they should return to the Lotus-eaters and be lost to their comrades for ever. Then with all speed he ordered the ships to set sail again, before any more of his men should taste of the fruit of the lotus and forget their homes.

The next land that they reached was the country of the Cyclopes, a simple, savage folk, of more than human size, who never tilled their land, or built ships or houses, or traded with other nations. Instead they lived in caves in the rocks and spent their time pasturing their flocks on their rich green fields.

Just off the mainland lay a wooded island, the home of many wild goats, and to this island the twelve ships came on a misty night. The men disembarked and slept; and in the morning, when the mist had cleared, they saw opposite them the land of the Cyclopes, and were surprised, for in the fog they had not imagined the mainland to be so close.

All that day they rested from their labours on the sea and feasted on the flesh of the island goats. Keeping a careful watch upon the land, Odysseus was just able to make out the huge flocks of sheep and the cattle of the Cyclopes, browsing in the fields, and the smoke from the fires of the herdsmen. 'Tomorrow', he said, 'I shall go with one ship to the mainland and see who lives in that rich country. It may well be a friendly folk who will give us welcome hospitality after our days at sea.'

Accordingly, in the morning Odysseus sailed to the mainland and beached his ship on the shore below a rocky cliff which towered above their heads, with shrubs growing among the rocks and little yellow wallflowers springing from every cleft.

Close by, half-way up the cliff and approached by a zigzag pathway, was the opening of a wide cave, half-hidden by laurel bushes and surrounded by a wall of huge stones. It was plain to see that the cave was someone's home, and picking out twelve of his best men, Odysseus set off up the cliff carrying a skin of the finest wine he had on board, as a gift for whoever might live there.

Beyond the wall they found a courtyard with pens for sheep and goats; though the pens were empty when they saw them, for the flocks were out at pasture with their owner.

'There is no one here,' said Odysseus. 'Let us wait in the cave for the shepherd to return.' And they passed beneath the glossy foliage of the overhanging laurels and went inside.

Within, the light was dim, but when their eyes grew used to it, they saw that the huge cave held many pens of lambs and kids, all separated according to their ages. There were, too, great pails of milk, and cheeses stacked in baskets hanging from the roof. But for all this abundance of good food the cave did not seem a friendly place, and Odysseus' men urged him to let them take as many cheeses and lambs as they could carry and return at once to the ship. But he would not hear of this. 'We could not rob a stranger in his absence,' he said. 'Besides, when he returns it may please him to give us far more gifts than thirteen men can carry off, and it would be folly to miss the chance of filling our ship with savoury cheeses and tender kids which we might share with our comrades waiting on the island.'

So they remained in the cave, and towards evening the herdsman returned with his flocks. He was as tall as three men and broad, with but one eye in the middle of his forehead; and as soon as Odysseus and his men caught sight of him, they knew that they had been unwise to wait.

He came to the entrance of the cave and flung inside a huge bundle of logs, large branches lopped from tall pines and oaks, as faggots for his fire; and in terror the Greeks fled to the darkest corner of the cave and hid themselves. The monster penned his rams and goats in the courtyard.

and drove the ewes and she-goats into the cave for milking, blocking the entrance with a great stone. And even his sheep and goats were larger than any Odysseus had ever seen before.

When the milking was over, the monster penned the ewes with their lambs and the goats with their kids, and set himself to make a fire from the wood he had brought home. As soon as he had a blaze, he was able to see, by the light of the leaping flames, Odysseus and his men, crouching in the very farthest corner. 'Who are you, strangers?' he asked in a voice like thunder.

For all his terror Odysseus stepped forward and answered boldly enough. 'We are Greeks, sailing home to Ithaca from the war with Troy. The winds have carried us somewhat from our course, and we have come to you in the hope that you may be our host until we can set sail once more.'

The giant roared, 'I am Polyphemus the Cyclops, and I entertain no guests unless it pleases me. But tell me this, where have you beached your ship? Is she close by?'

Odysseus suspected the question and guessed the Cyclops meant harm to his ship and the men guarding her, and he answered cunningly, 'Our ship was wrecked upon your shore, and only I and these twelve men escaped alive from the sea.'

But Polyphemus gave no word of sympathy in reply. Instead, he seized a man in each hand, and dashing out their brains against the rocky floor, he tore them in pieces and ate them for his supper before the eyes of their horrified comrades. Then after drinking several large pailfuls of milk, he lay down by the fire to sleep.

Odysseus would have drawn his sword and crept upon him while he slept and killed him, but that he knew it would be impossible for him and his men to move away by themselves the great stone that blocked the opening of the cave. So, terrified, they waited all night, whispering together and trying to devise some means of outwitting the cruel monster.

At dawn Polyphemus rekindled the fire and milked his ewes and goats again. That done, he snatched up two more of Odysseus' men and ate them as a wild beast might have done. Then he rolled aside the great stone from the mouth of the cave and drove out his flocks; and replacing the stone once more, he went towards the mountain pastures, whistling cheerfully at the thought of the good supper which awaited his return.

Odysseus and the eight men left to him sat down beside the fire to think how they might escape the fate which would surely be theirs unless they could find a way to leave the cave; and at last a plan came to Odysseus. In the cave there lay a long pole of green olive-wood, drying so that it might serve the Cyclops for a staff. From this pole Odysseus hacked off with his sword a piece the length of a tall man, and set his companions to sharpen one end into a point and harden it in the fire.

'Tonight,' he said, 'when the monster sleeps, we will heat the wood red-hot and with it put out his single eye.'

When the point of the stake was hard and sharp, they hid it, and then chose by lot the four men who should help Odysseus use it in the night.

When evening came the Cyclops returned with his flocks, and this time he drove all the sheep into the cave, rams and ewes alike, and penned them safely. When he had milked the ewes and goats he thought of his own supper, and seized two more men. While he sat by the fire eating them, Odysseus poured out a huge bowlful of the wine he had brought with him, and coming forward, offered it to Polyphemus. 'Such wine as this our ship held before it was wrecked upon your shores,' he said. 'Come, taste of it and tell me if you think it is not good.'

The Cyclops took the wooden bowl and drained it at one draught. He held it out to Odysseus. 'Give me more,' he said.

Odysseus filled it a second time, and again the monster drank. 'Give me yet more of your wine, stranger,' he demanded, 'and tell me your name, that I may give you a gift in return.'

A third time Odysseus filled the bowl and the Cyclops drank. 'My name is No-one,' said Odysseus. 'Tell me now what gift you will give to No-one in exchange for his good wine.'

'I will eat you last of all your comrades. A few more hours of life, that shall be my gift to you.' And with a mighty laugh that echoed through the cave Polyphemus lay down beside the fire; and made drowsy by the wine, he fell deeply asleep at once.

Odysseus thrust the stake into the embers and held it there until it was red-hot, then taking it, he and the four men on whom the lot had fallen drove it deep into the Cyclops' eye.

With screams and with shouts of rage Polyphemus awoke and pulled the stake from the socket of his eye, and wildly flinging his arms about and stumbling around the cave, he tried to catch Odysseus and his friends, who crouched trembling against the wall.

The neighbouring Cyclopes who dwelt in caverns nearby heard his cries, and coming to his cave, stood outside the great stone and called to him. 'What ails you, Polyphemus? Why do you wake us with your cries? Does someone steal your sheep or kill you?'

'Good neighbours,' said Polyphemus, 'it is the cunning wiles of No-one that are killing me.'

'If no one is killing you,' answered the neighbours, 'you must be sick, and illness comes from the gods, and we can be of no help to you. You have woken us in vain. May your sickness have left you by the morning.' And they returned to their own homes.

But the Cyclops groped his way to the entrance of the cave and pushed away the great stone, and sitting down in the doorway, waited to catch any of the men who might try to pass him; so that they saw that there was no escape for them that way.

At the far end of the cave Odysseus and his companions made whispered plans; and taking reeds from Polyphemus' bed, Odysseus bound together eighteen of the finest rams in threes, with one of his six men tied beneath each middle ram. Then he himself laid hold of the largest ram of all, a great creature with a splendid fleece, and lay underneath it, clinging on and hidden by the shaggy wool that hung down from its broad sides.

By that time it was dawn, and the rams were eager to be grazing in the rich pastures. Bleating, they moved together to the entrance of the cave, where Polyphemus felt across the back of each one as it came to him, before passing it through into the courtyard. But he never thought to feel beneath the animals, so the six men went safely out. Last of all to come was the leader of the flock, walking slowly under the weight of Odysseus, clinging to its fleece.

As Polyphemus felt its back he spoke to it. 'My good ram, you are ever the foremost of the flock, leading the others to their grazing ground. Why are you last today? Are you grieved for your master, blinded by wicked No-one, and would stay to comfort him? I would that you could speak and tell me where he hides, that wretch who took away my sight. But go, dear ram, join your companions in the fields.' And Polyphemus moved his hand aside and the ram stepped through the opening into the sunlight, bearing Odysseus.

Once outside the courtyard, Odysseus freed himself from his hiding-place and went to release his companions. Then hastily they drove the sheep down to the ship and their comrades waiting on the shore. With no delay they stowed the flock on board and set out to row back to the island where the fleet was moored.

A little way from the shore Odysseus stood up in the ship and shouted with all his might, 'Now indeed, wicked Cyclops, do you know what ills your cruelty to helpless strangers has brought to you.'

Polyphemus heard him and came out from his cave in fury, and breaking off a huge piece of rock he flung it into the sea in the direction of Odysseus' voice. It fell in the water by the bows and the great waves made by its fall washed the ship back towards the shore; but Odysseus seized a long pole and pushed off again, and his men fell to rowing hard once more.

Again Odysseus stood up to shout his taunts to the Cyclops, and though his men tried to restrain him, for they feared another rock might be cast at them, he called out, 'Polyphemus, if anyone should ever ask you how you lost your sight, you may tell him that Odysseus, king of Ithaca, put out your eye.'

And Polyphemus cried out with a loud voice, 'Alas, it was foretold that great grief would come to me through Odysseus, king of Ithaca, but I had thought he would be a fine big man, a worthy enemy for me, not a tiny weakling like yourself. But evil will come to you as well from this, for Poseidon, god of the sea whereon you sail, is my father, and he will avenge my eye.' And he held out his hands over the water and prayed to his father for vengeance. 'Great Poseidon, lord of all the seas, grant your son this one request. May Odysseus and his men never reach their home in Ithaca. But if, in spite of all his misdeeds, it is the will of the gods that Odysseus should gain the shores of his own land, let it be alone and friendless, and may he find sorrow awaiting him in his house.'

And again Polyphemus tore off and hurled into the sea a rock. But this time it fell to the stern of the ship, and sent her rushing forward to the island.

Once safely with the men from his other ships, Odysseus divided the sheep among them, a fair share to each. But his companions allotted him the fine ram by the help of which he had escaped, as an extra gift, because he was their leader and because he had saved six of his men from the Cyclops.

All that day they feasted on the island, and in the morning they set sail once more. But mighty Poseidon had heard the prayer of Polyphemus the Cyclops, and he brought great trouble on Odysseus and his men.

They came next to the floating island of Aeolia, around which ran a mighty wall of cliff surmounted by a wall of bronze, and within these brazen walls lay the lands of Aeolus, guardian of the winds. In his vast palace he lived with his wife and twelve children, six sons and six daughters, feasting continually. Every day on Aeolia was a holiday with banquets and rejoicing, abundant food and everflowing wine. And far from the palace could the savoury smells of roasting meats be marked, and the sounds of revelry.

Aeolus and his family welcomed Odysseus and his men with kindness and willing hospitality; and for thirty days they lived in the palace, joining in the feasting and gaiety of their hosts. At great length Odysseus related all the deeds of the Greeks at Troy; and there was no end to the questions that Aeolus asked of all that he had seen and done in the ten years after he had left his home in Ithaca.

Since Aeolus had all the winds of the world in his keeping, when the time came for Odysseus to depart, he asked his host for a favourable breeze, that his ships might reach the coast of Ithaca with all speed. Aeolus promised him a brisk west wind to make his voyage short, and gave him besides, all the contrary winds tied in a leathern sack; so that until the sack was opened when he was safely home, not one might blow and drive him from his course.

This sack Odysseus kept close beside him, never permitting any of his followers to touch it, nor telling them what it contained; until, on the tenth day after they had left Aeolia, the coast of Ithaca came in sight. Then indeed did

Odysseus and his men rejoice, when they came close enough to see the herdsmen's fires upon the hills; and then at last Odysseus relaxed his eager watching for the first sight of land, and lay down to rest. Thinking of his wife, Penelope, whom he had left ten years before with her tiny babe in her arms, he smiled, wondering if she would have altered in his absence; whether she was now as beautiful as a woman as she had been as a young maiden; and reflecting that the babe would now be a sturdy little boy of ten years old, to whom his father would seem a stranger. 'To see them both again,' thought Odysseus, 'could any joy be greater?' And thinking pleasantly of their happiness and of all he had to tell them, he fell asleep.

While their leader slept the men in Odysseus' ship talked. 'It will be good to see our homes again,' said one. 'And we have spoils in plenty to gladden our families.'

Another glanced at the leathern sack beside Odysseus. 'He has more than we,' he said.

'He is our king,' said another, 'it is only fitting that his portion should be greater.'

'Our voyage has been as long and perilous as his,' grumbled the man who had spoken second, 'but good Aeolus gave us nothing. That great sack Odysseus guards so carefully is doubtless filled with gold and silver; cups and platters and finely wrought bowls to hold the sparkling wine. I would that we had gifts as fine to carry home.'

And they stared at the sack until envy made them rash and they spoke foolishly. 'Let us open the sack and see what may be in it. Perchance there will be inside some small thing apiece for us which will not be missed.' And one of them opened the sack quietly to look inside, and all the winds rushed out, filling the sky and beating the sea into mighty waves and driving the ships back the way that they had come.

Odysseus awoke at the despairing cries of his men, to see the coast of Ithaca vanish from sight as the ships were borne swiftly towards the island of Aeolia.

Landing on Aeolia, Odysseus went with two men to the palace, to ask if Aeolus might not help him once again. He entered the hall where Aeolus feasted with his family and friends, and sitting down by the doorway he waited silently.

Aeolus saw him with amazement. 'Odysseus, how have you come here? I thought that by this day you would have been in your own home. Did I not make your return to Ithaca certain by my help?'

Then Odysseus told them what his comrades had done, and he pleaded, 'Give me your help once again, good Aeolus, for we are indeed the most miserable of men.'

But Aeolus and his sons rose up and drove him from the hall, saying, 'Go from the island instantly, for you must be the unluckiest of all mortals, and carry ill fortune wherever you set foot. Begone, for we want here no bringers of calamity.'

And Odysseus and his ships put out to sea once more, and this time Aeolus kept the winds prisoned on the island and the sea was calm; so calm that for six days and nights the men were forced to row unceasingly.

On the seventh day they reached Telepylus, the home of the Laestrygonians. In this land there was no night, but the sun shone unendingly; so that a man who needed no sleep could have earned two men's wages, as a shepherd by day, and as a cowherd during the sunlit night.

In Telepylus they found a fine harbour, a cliff curving around like a horn on either side of it, with a narrow passage out to sea. In this calm bay eleven of Odysseus' ships moored, so that the men might have rest after their toil at the oars. But Odysseus made fast his ship at the point of one of the curving horns of land, for he wished to climb the cliff to see if he could gain a glimpse of the inhabitants of the country.

From the topmost rock of the cliff all he could see was the smoke from a few fires; no dwellings, no herds, no men. So he sent out three of his followers to bring back tidings of the Laestrygonians, and of their chances of finding in that land the provisions they needed, and perhaps news of a kindly host to welcome them at his house.

The three men found a well-made road leading from the shore, and a little way along it they met a maiden, tall and handsome, drawing water from a spring. They asked her who was king of the land and where he lived, and she replied, 'My father is King Antiphates and yonder is his house.' And she led them to a lofty building near a town of great houses, the largest they had ever seen. In the house a woman of enormous size, Antiphates' queen, came to them, and with fair words beguiled them and made them sit and eat, while she sent for her husband to come home at once.

Already filled with fear at the sight of the queen, who seemed to them to be as tall as a mountain, the three men were struck with terror at the appearance of King Antiphates, striding into his halls with a mighty roar, for he was even taller than his wife.

Immediately he seized one of the unfortunate men, and

killing him with one blow, tossed him to his wife. 'Make him ready for my supper,' he said.

Before he could catch them also, the two others rose and fled back to where Odysseus waited by his ship, but almost before they could stammer out their story, Antiphates had called up his men; and standing on the cliffs the Laestrygonians hurled great rocks upon the ships, pent up in the harbour and unable to pass with any speed through the narrow way to the open sea beyond. The timbers of the ships were shattered and the men struggled in the water, seeking to reach the safety of the shore before they drowned. But the giants rushed down to the beach and speared them as they swam and carried them in triumph to their homes to cook and eat.

Seeing that there was no way of saving the remainder of his ships from the Laestrygonians, Odysseus cut through the cables of his own ship with his sword and shouted to his men to row out to sea with all their might; and thus he saved them from the slaughter.

But of all his fleet that had sailed so joyfully from Troy, that one ship alone was saved.

II

Circe

ODYSSEUS and his companions sailed on, glad to have escaped alive from the cruel Laestrygonians, but with their hearts heavy for their slain comrades. After many days they sighted the shores of Aeaea, a fair green island in the waste of blue sea.

Thankful to be within reach of land again, they put in to the shore at a spot where the coastline made a safe harbour for the ship, and cast themselves down upon the golden sand, weary and dispirited. For two days and two nights they sighed and sorrowed for their friends whom they had lost, and for the homes and families they feared they might never see again; and Odysseus, as full of grief as any of his men, sat crouched beside a rock, his cloak drawn across his face.

But it was not Odysseus' way to remain long inactive

and despairing; and on the morning of the third day, when he saw the sun rise in a blaze of rosy light, making a golden path across the sea from the far horizon to the very shore where he lay, he jumped to his feet, flinging aside his sluggardly sorrow with his cloak. 'For shame,' he thought, 'shall I remain here idle while there are yet things which I could do to help my men?' And taking his sword and his spear he turned his back upon the sea and walked away to where the beach sloped upwards towards a hill, thinking that from this higher land he might gain a sight of the island and perhaps judge what manner of people dwelt upon it.

He climbed hopefully up the rocky hillside where the little pink cyclamen with their silver-mottled leaves untwisted their buds in the morning sunlight; and at the top he stood and looked out across the whole isle. He saw that inland of the rocky hills that ran around the coast, Aeaea was a pleasant wooded valley.

As his sharp eyes wandered over the treetops, Odysseus suddenly caught sight of a streak of blue-grey smoke that rose up through the trees into the calm morning air. 'Where there is smoke', he said to himself, 'there is a hearth; and where there is a hearth, there someone has his home; though what manner of man he may be, whether friendly to strangers or of ill intent, no one may guess.' And he wondered in his mind whether to go alone among the tall trees to spy out the chances of friendly entertainment, or to return to the shore and rouse his men, and bid them come with him into the wood.

But while he stood undecided, he saw a fine stag step from the shelter of the trees to drink at a little stream which ran below him. His heart leapt up at the sight. 'Fresh meat', he thought, 'will put new courage into my men. A good meal will make them bold once more.' And carefully and silently he poised his spear and hurled it at the beast. His aim was perfect and the stag fell dead. Rejoicing, Odysseus ran down the slope; and plucking reeds from the banks of the stream, and cutting pliant branches from a nearby willow, he plaited a strong rope with which he tied the legs of the stag together, and heaved the animal across his shoulders. With his burden he climbed slowly to the top of the hill, and from there descended once again to the shore.

He woke his men with a great shout, and when they saw the stag they came running eagerly. 'Come, my friends,' said Odysseus, 'let us not give way to grief while we yet have good food to eat. Let us feast and regain our courage.'

Soon a fire had been lit on the beach and the venison was roasting over it. Wine was brought from the ship in painted jars and skins, and Odysseus and his men spread out their cloaks upon the sand and sat down to eat and drink. All that day they feasted and rejoiced, and that night they slept peacefully and free from grief.

In the morning early, Odysseus called his companions together and told them of the smoke he had seen rising above the treetops beyond the hill. 'We must go', he said, 'and see who lives in the wood. Perhaps we may meet with some hospitable folk who will give us food and drink and beds to sleep upon at night, until we feel ourselves able to set sail once more for Ithaca.'

Most of his men were fearful of what the wood might hide, for they remembered the Laestrygonians and the terrible Cyclops; but Odysseus was insistent, and dividing his followers into two bands of twenty-two men each, he put one group under the leadership of Eurylochus, whose courage he trusted, and remained himself in charge of the other. Then with black and white pebbles from the beach in a helmet, they drew lots to decide who should stay by the ship, and who should undertake the journey to the wood. And it fell to the lot of Eurylochus and his party to go, while Odysseus remained on the shore.

With grief and foreboding the comrades took leave of each other, and Eurylochus and his two-and-twenty followers climbed the hill from the beach and descended to the wood on the other side in the direction Odysseus had pointed out to them. Then they too saw the smoke rising against the blue sky from among the trees, as he had described; and unwillingly they entered the wood.

After a time they came upon a clearing where stood a large house of polished stone: wide rooms on three sides about a courtyard, with a flat roof above and a handsome entrance porch.

'It is a fine house,' they said, 'it might well be the home of kindly folk.' And they left the shelter of the trees and crossed the clearing towards the house.

But half-way across the open space they paused in horror, for from round about the building there leapt towards them a pack of shaggy wolves with several great tawny lions in their midst, and in a moment Eurylochus and his companions were surrounded by the beasts.

'Surely we shall perish here', they thought, 'and never see again our good ship or Odysseus, our king.'

But to their astonishment the wolves fawned upon them

like eager dogs, jumping up to greet them and howling a welcome with wagging tails; while the lions purred like cats and rubbed huge yellow-maned heads against their shoulders. But friendly as the animals seemed to be, they were yet wolves and lions, and the men were afraid.

'Let us seek safety in the house,' shouted Eurylochus; and without further thought than to escape from the wild beasts surrounding them, the men ran to the shelter of the doorway. The lions and wolves did not follow them there, and as the twenty-three comrades stood huddled together, they could hear, from within the house, the sound of a woman singing. Her voice was young and beautiful, and her sweet song brought courage to their frightened hearts.

Then Polites, one of Odysseus' bravest captains, spoke: 'Whoever she is who sings within the house, her voice would not disgrace one of the immortal goddesses. No woman with a voice like that could have an evil heart. Let us call to her and ask her hospitality.'

To this suggestion they were all agreed save Eurylochus, who strove to persuade them against the risk of entering an unknown house without finding out more about her who dwelt in it than that she could sing sweetly. But no one heeded him; it was as though the song had robbed them of their wits, and they called out loudly to whoever was inside the house; and instantly the singing ceased and the great doors opened.

A lovely woman in a bright robe stood upon the threshold. Her hair was divided and curled into seven locks and braided with purple ribbons; and her red lips parted in a smile of welcome. 'Come in, strangers,' she said. 'This is Circe's home. Come in and enjoy the hospitality of

Circe.' And she stood aside to let them pass, and led by Polites, the men entered her house eagerly, all but Eurylochus, and the doors closed behind them. But Eurylochus was afraid and hid behind a fig-tree that grew beside the porch.

Circe led her guests into the great hall of her house, furnished with chairs and couches of costly woods and precious metals, and she bade them sit while she brought them food and wine. They sat on the comfortable chairs and lay on the couches covered with the many-coloured cloths woven by Circe herself on her great loom, and congratulated each other on their wise decision to call to the fair singer for admittance to her home. But they did not know that Circe was an enchantress whose delight it was to turn men into animals—the wolves and lions that prowled around the clearing had once been men—and that they themselves were to be her next victims.

She brought them barley cakes with honey, and red wine in silver cups, and bade them eat and drink, and smiled at them. But with the wine she had mixed an evil drug which caused them to forget the land where they had been born and once lived happily. And when they had eaten and drunk, she rose and took her magic wand and struck with it each man in turn, and one after another, they were changed into swine.

Then Circe drove them out into the courtyard and penned them in the sty, two-and-twenty swine but with yet their own human minds to deplore their plight, and their own human hearts to sorrow at their fate. She flung among them handfuls of acorn and beech nuts, the favourite food of pigs; and for all their human minds they scrambled for them, grunting and trampling on each other in their eagerness. And Circe laughed.

Hidden beside the porch, Eurylochus listened, and when he could no longer hear the murmur of voices from within, his fears increased; and after there had been silence in the house for a great while, he fled across the clearing, through the woods, and back to where Odysseus waited on the shore. There he related all that had happened since he and his companions had set off; how they had reached the house in the wood and how the animals had greeted them, and how the others had all entered the house and he had seen no more of them.

Odysseus buckled on his sword. 'Lead me back to the spot where stands this house,' he said, 'and I will discover, if I can, what has become of our friends.'

But Eurylochus fell upon his knees in fearful dismay and pleaded, 'Do not ask me to go back with you to that terrible place, for I am sure that our comrades have perished; as you yourself will also perish if you go to seek for them. Let us instead set sail from this unlucky island while there are still some of us left alive.'

But Odysseus answered firmly, 'I cannot desert my men while they may yet be living. Stay here by the ship, Eurylochus, and eat and drink to keep up your courage and strength, and I will go alone.' And he turned and went over the hill and down into the wood, while Eurylochus and the other men sat on the beach beside their ship and mourned him as one already lost, for they never thought to see him again.

Odysseus hurried through the wood, wondering what terrors his quest would bring to him; and among the trees there came to him Hermes, the swift messenger of the immortal gods, in the guise of a lovely youth.

'Greetings, unfortunate Odysseus,' he said. 'Have you come to free your comrades from the enchantments of the sorceress Circe? I fear that, unaided, you will fail, for her magic is powerful, and your men are turned to grunting swine and penned up in her sty. There you will surely join them if you lack my help. But I will give you a strong charm against her witchcraft and tell you what you must do. She will speak kindly to you and ask you to enter her house, and after she has given you food and drink into which she has put her evil drugs, she will strike you with her magic wand, that you may take the shape of a beast. But with my charm to help you, her spells will have no power over you. And when she touches you with her wand you must rise and draw your sword and make as though you meant to kill her. She will plead with you for her life and ask you to remain with her and offer you friendship and hospitality. Do not refuse her offers, but threaten her until she swears she means no evil to you, for otherwise she will surely do you harm when you lie helpless and asleep within her house.' And Hermes bent and plucked up from the ground a little plant with a twisted black root and flowers as white as milk. 'This plant is moly,' he said, 'a very potent charm against all evil.' And he gave it to Odysseus, and in the next instant he was gone.

Wondering, Odysseus went on towards the house, and standing in the porch he heard Circe within, singing as she moved to and fro before her great loom, weaving the bright-patterned cloth. He called to her and at once the singing ceased and the doors opened and Circe stood there, smiling. 'You are welcome, stranger,' she said. 'This is Circe's home. Come in and enjoy the hospitality of Circe.' And she stood aside and Odysseus entered the house, and she closed the doors behind him.

Filled with apprehension he followed her, and she bade him sit upon a chair of rare wood inlaid with silver and placed a footstool at his feet. She gave him wine mixed with her evil drugs in a golden cup; and when he had drunk she struck him with her wand. 'Go now and join your comrades in the sty,' she ordered.

But as Hermes had said, the little plant moly was a powerful charm, and Circe's spells had no effect on Odysseus. Instead, as he had been bidden, he leapt to his feet and drew his sword and rushed upon the enchantress.

She gave a great cry and fell at his feet, begging him to spare her life. 'What manner of man are you,' she asked in amazement, 'that my magic has no power over you? Surely you can be no other than the wise Odysseus, famed for his cunning and skill, whom Hermes once prophesied should come one day to my house. If you are indeed Odysseus, then I wish you no harm. Sheathe your sword and stay here with me in trust and friendship, an honoured guest, for as long as you will.'

But Odysseus replied, 'There can be no trust between us, Circe, until you have sworn an oath to plan no evil deeds against me. And how can I give friendship to one who has tricked my men and laid a wicked enchantment on them, and would without a doubt do the same to me as soon as there was an opportunity?'

So Circe swore a solemn oath that she meant no harm to Odysseus, and he put aside his sword.

And Circe called the four maidens who served her and bade them minister to Odysseus as befitted such a noble guest. One of them heated water in a brazen cauldron that he might bathe himself, and took from him his travel-stained garments and gave him instead a new tunic of finest linen and a warm cloak. Another spread the chairs with purple-dyed cloth and laid rugs upon the floor; and the third brought little silver tables to set beside the chairs; while the fourth mixed sweet wine in a silver bowl.

Odysseus sat in the chair of silver-inlaid wood and the four serving-maids brought him wine and bread and choice meats on golden dishes; but he was sad at heart for his comrades, penned in the sty, and he could not eat or drink.

And when Circe saw that he would touch neither food nor wine, she thought that he yet mistrusted her, and she came and stood beside him and asked, 'Why will you not eat of my food and drink my crimson wine, Odysseus? Is it because you suspect me of some treachery? You do me wrong, for have I not sworn an oath to harm you not?'

Odysseus sighed and answered her, 'Can a man eat who grieves for his friends, turned to swine and herded in a sty? If you truly wish me well and would see me enjoy your food and wine, release my dear comrades from your enchantment.'

And Circe went from the hall with her wand, taking with her a little jar of magic ointment. She opened the doors of the sty and the unhappy swine rushed forth into the courtyard, and Circe went among them and anointed each one of them with the ointment, and in an instant he became a man as he had been before. One after another they ran to Odysseus and greeted him with tears of joy;

and their mingled laughter and weeping filled the hall, so that even Circe was moved by the relief and happiness of her former victims.

Then Circe spoke to Odysseus, saying, 'Go now and call your other men from the beach, where they wait beside the ship, that they may also eat and drink with us.'

So Odysseus went himself to the shore, for he thought that his men might be hard to convince of Circe's well-wishing after the fears they had had of her. As indeed they were.

They saw him approach and gathered round with wondering welcome, for they had thought never to see him again. When he told them of all that had passed and how with the help of Hermes he had prevailed and overcome the powers of the enchantress, they rejoiced. But when he told them that Circe awaited them with food and wine and the hospitality of her home, they were afraid.

But in the end Odysseus persuaded them, and at last they believed that there was no longer anything to fear from the wiles of the sorceress, and they began to drag the ship up on to the beach and stow away the tackle in a nearby cave. All save Eurylochus, who, because he had once been to Circe's house, dared not go again, and sought to warn his comrades against trusting Odysseus' reassuring words.

'My friends,' he said, 'if you rely upon Odysseus who is rash and adventurous and go to the house of Circe, you will not return. Rather will she change you into swine or lions or shaggy wolves to guard her home. Do you not remember how six of our companions, who went with him into the Cyclops' cave, paid for his rashness with their lives?'

But Odysseus' men trusted him. Besides, they were weary and longed for the comforts of a house after their labours on the sea, and they replied, 'Good Odysseus, we will go with you to Circe's home. But if it pleases you, let us leave Eurylochus to guard the ship, since he is afraid to come with us.'

And with that they followed Odysseus over the hill and into the wood. And Eurylochus went after them, for he had no wish to earn his king's displeasure.

III

The Land of Hades

FOR a year Odysseus and his comrades remained in Circe's house, feasting and enjoying the comforts of idleness; but when a full twelve months were passed, the men grew restless, and besought Odysseus to remember Ithaca, their home.

'For still we long to see our wives and families and the shores of our own country,' they reminded him. 'Let us not stay here for ever, pleasant though it is to pass the days in luxury and ease.'

So Odysseus went to Circe and told her of what his men had said, and asked her favour for his voyage and her counsel as to how best to act that they might return in safety to their homes. 'For,' he said, 'we have had ill luck with our voyaging since we sailed from Troy, and we need guidance.'

'My favour for your voyage shall I give you willingly,' she said. 'But even I cannot tell you what the future holds for you. For that you must go to the land of Hades, the god who rules the spirits of all the dead, and ask counsel from Teiresias, the blind prophet. While he yet lived, Teiresias was the greatest seer in all the world, and still in death he has no equal.'

In astonishment and horror Odysseus cried out, 'But how shall I, a living man, reach Hades' land? No man has ever yet sailed his ship into the realms of the god of the dead.'

'You need have no fear, Odysseus, for you will be guided on the way. Put out to sea with your destination boldly in your mind, and the north wind will bear you over the water to the River of Oceanus in the land of the Cimmerians. There must you beach your ship and walk inland to where two of Hades' rivers, Periphlegethon and Cocytus, meet and flow on into Acheron, a third and greater river. There, at that place, sacrifice a ram and a black ewe to the memory of all the dead, and call upon the spirit of Teiresias. Then wait, and shortly he will come to you and tell you all you seek to know.'

At dawn the next day, Odysseus roused his men and told them that the time had come for them to sail once more, and great indeed was their joy when they heard his words. But their rejoicing was turned to grief when they learnt that it was not to Ithaca, but to the land of Hades, that they were to voyage first. But for all their misgivings, they stirred themselves to make ready for the journey with a will; though ill fortune came to one of the company, Elpenor, the youngest of them all, a simple youth and none too skilled at fighting. For he had climbed up on to the flat roof of Circe's house to sleep, the night being warm; and in the morning, hearing his comrades' shouts as they prepared to go down to the shore, he rose up hastily, forgetting where he was, and ran to go to them; and he fell from the roof and his neck was broken.

Down on the beach, Odysseus' men dragged the ship out from the cave where they had hidden her, twelve months before. They went over her timbers carefully, to see that none had decayed; and swept off the deck the sand that had collected there, having been blown into the cave by the winds from the sea. They tested the ropes of plaited oxhide that went to make the rigging, to be sure that they would still hold against a storm; and they brushed cobwebs off the sail.

With ropes fastened to her blue-painted bow, they drew the ship down to the water's edge, and there they stepped the mast, securing it with the forestays and the backstays. Then, with a final push into the sea, they clambered on board, and falling to their oars, rowed her out into the deeper water. There, hauling on the halyard, they hoisted the yard; and then unfurled the sail, trimming it to the wind. And it was even as Circe had said, and a fresh breeze from the north filled the square white sail, and the ship sped over the sea without guidance from the helmsman.

And so Odysseus and his men came to the River of Oceanus at the ends of the earth in the country of the Cimmerians, who dwelt all their days in mist and fog, never seeing the golden sunlight or the silver rays of the moon.

A little way up the river they beached the ship and went inland through the groves of Persephone, among the tall straight poplars with their ever-rustling leaves, and the mournful drooping willows, until they reached the spot Circe had told Odysseus of. Here, with a swirling of dark waters, Periphlegethon, the river that flashed like fire, and Cocytus, the river of wailing, mingled their streams and flowed on into melancholy Acheron.

In this place Odysseus paused; and helped by Eurylochus and another of his men, he dug a pit the width of a single pace across both ways. Into this pit he poured out an offering to the dead of milk and honey, wine, water, and white barley flour; and sacrificed a ram and a black ewe, which Circe had given him; and called upon Teiresias.

At once the spirits of the dead appeared, and foremost of their company came the spirit of Elpenor, who had fallen from the roof of Circe's house at dawn. He had not yet been buried, for his comrades had been in such haste to embark from Aeaea that they had not spared the time to build his funeral pyre, meaning to do so later, on their return to the island.

He now came forward, looking as he had ever done in life, young, and a little puzzled, and eagerly he made towards Odysseus.

Seeing him, Odysseus was filled with grief, and asked him sadly, saying, 'Elpenor, my friend, how have you come here, all among the darkness, in this place of gloom? Truly, you have reached here more quickly, travelling on foot, than the rest of us, in our swift ship.'

Elpenor gave a great sigh, and answered, 'King Odysseus, my good and noble leader, an ill fate overtook me, for when I came to climb down from Circe's roof, in my eagerness to join my dear comrades, I forgot to go to the

K·M

ladder, and I fell. With speed my spirit left my body and I came hence, even to the land of Hades, god of all the dead; and here, now, shall I ever remain. But you, King Odysseus, and all my other companions with you, will depart from this place and return to Aeaea. There, I beg of you, remember me, and do not sail for Ithaca leaving me unlamented and unburied. Build a barrow for me on the shore of the sea, and set upon it my oar with which I rowed in our ship, that men may not forget me utterly. I ask you this in the name of all those whom you love and left behind in Ithaca. In the name of good Lord Laertes, your father, and in the name of your fair queen, Penelope, and for the sake of your little son, to whom you will one day return. In their name do this for me, Odysseus, and do not forsake me.'

With tears Odysseus replied to him, 'I promise you, Elpenor, my unlucky friend, that we shall not forget you. All this shall we do for you, even as you say.'

Then, satisfied by the promise, the spirit of Elpenor drifted away, and from the midst of the great throng of spirits, stepped forth the spirit of Teiresias, the prophet, bearing a golden staff.

'You seek knowledge from me of your return to Ithaca, Odysseus?' he asked. 'Indeed, your return shall be long deferred, for you angered Poseidon, great lord of the seas, when you blinded his son, Polyphemus the Cyclops. Yet if you have a care, you will once again see your own land, in spite of Poseidon's wrath. But take heed if on your voyage home you should chance to light upon the island of Thrinacia and see there the herds and flocks of Helios, who rules the rising and the setting of the sun. Do not harm them, or your men will all be lost, and you yourself, if you should have the good fortune to escape, will only reach your home after many perils, alone and in the ship of another man; while in your own house you will find strife, and strangers despoiling your possessions. But in the end, Odysseus, whatever your misfortunes, it is fated that you will be avenged on all your enemies, and your old age shall be spent in peace and comfort in your home, with your own people all about you.'

With this the spirit of the prophet vanished, and the other spirits crowded round. Amongst them Odysseus recognized many whom he had known in the days of their life on earth; men who had fought beside him at Troy, and died there, and others whom he had known when young; and with them the spirit of his mother, Anticleia, whom he had thought still lived.

He called to her, 'Dear mother, tell me, how came you here?'

'My son,' she replied, 'I pined, and died of a broken heart, because you were so long away from home.'

'And my father, Laertes, has he too come to Hades' land?'

'Your princely father lives, my child, but in a wretched state, unfitted to his rank. He has gone from your house to his farm in the country, where in rags and patches he toils all day in the fields, like a common bondman, ever grieving for you and longing for your return. At night, in the winter, he sleeps in the ashes by the hearth, along with the slaves; and in the summer, he rests on a bed of fallen leaves, down by his vineyard. And always he sorrows for you.'

And Odysseus wept and said, 'My poor unhappy father,'

and he made to take his mother in his arms and kiss her, but her misty spirit flittered through his hands as though she had been a dream that is forgotten on awaking, or an insubstantial shadow, lost because a cloud has hidden the sun. Three times he tried, and three times she was not there. 'Dear mother,' he cried, 'may I not touch you?'

'Indeed no, my son,' she said, 'for I dwell now in Hades' land, while you still belong to the world of sunlight and the living. Farewell, dear child.' And so she went, and her voice died away.

When his mother had gone from him, Odysseus spoke with the spirits of many others; great ladies of the past, and his former comrades of the war with Troy, who pressed round eagerly, glad to speak with him again.

Among them was Agamemnon, mighty leader of all the Greeks at Troy, who on his return to his palace in the broad lands of Argos had been treacherously slain by his cousin Aegisthus, in vengeance for an old family quarrel.

'Unfortunate Agamemnon,' said Odysseus when he had heard the story, 'what an ill-starred home-coming there was for you.'

'But one day for you, Odysseus,' replied the spirit of great King Agamemnon, 'will there be a happy reunion with your wife and family. For among your loved ones, as I remember them, there are none who would strike you down by stealth.'

There came also to Odysseus the spirit of golden-haired Achilles, with his dear friend Patroclus by his side. They had both been slain at Troy in all the glory of their youth. And after them came Antilochus, who had been old King Nestor's son.

'Odysseus,' asked Achilles, as the other spirits gave way to him, 'why have you, still living, come among us here?'

'I came to ask counsel of Teiresias, for my voyage home to Ithaca has been ill fated since the day I sailed from Troy. Truly, I am a most unlucky man, and I could envy you, Achilles. You were a great prince while you yet lived, and even here, in Hades' land, you are still honoured and respected.'

But Achilles sighed. 'No, my friend,' he said, 'I would rather be on earth, alive, the slave of some poor wretched man, and live in drudgery and want, than rule here, king of all the dead. But what of my son, Odysseus? He was only a child when last I saw him; but when he grew older, did he fight with you at Troy?'

'Neoptolemus, your son, is very young, Achilles, but he is wise beyond his years, and he has inherited his father's valour. Indeed, when he came to Troy, there was none who would press forward in the fight so fast as he, or rush so eagerly to battle. For all his lack of age, he was among the bravest of us there. This will show you what manner of youth he is. In the tenth year of the siege, when it seemed to us as though we never should take Troy by storm, we decided to achieve our ends by stealth. We fashioned a huge horse of wood, cunningly carved, and running on wheels, but all hollow within. This horse we left upon the plain before the city; and then, with a great show of men and arms and ships, we set sail, so that the Trojans might think the siege had been abandoned. Then, in the darkness, one ship sailed back, and in it was the pick of all the Grecian army. We crept across the plain to the wooden horse and climbed inside; and in the morning the Trojans came, and thinking it an offering to the gods which we had left behind, they dragged it towards the city, and opened to it the gates that had been closed to us for nigh on ten years. Prisoned within the wooden walls we tarried until nightfall, when we might steal forth and fall upon the Trojans. All through that day of weary waiting many stout hearts faltered, and there were among us some who wished they had not been chosen for the task of taking Troy. But not your son, Achilles. In the dim light of our prison young Neoptolemus delayed impatiently, his sword clasped firmly in his hand. And to me, to whom the charge had been given to say the word when we should break from our hiding-place, he would ever whisper eagerly, "It must be dusk, Odysseus, let us go forth," and, "We have been here a lifetime, how much longer must we wait?" Indeed, Achilles, your son knows not fear.'

There came a smile to the lips of Achilles' spirit and his eyes grew bright, and without another word he turned and went with Patroclus, walking lightly and joyously away, across the dim fields of Hades' land, scattered with the amber-striped pale stars of the little asphodel.

And many were the questions asked of Odysseus by the other spirits who drew near; until at last he returned to his ship and he and his companions rowed down the River of Oceanus to the sea, and sailed once more for Aeaea.

There, on the shore of Circe's isle, they built a pyre of logs, strong oak and beech and resin-scented pine, and on it they laid the body of Elpenor, with his armour and his sword, and Odysseus fired the pile with a flaming torch. They stood by, sorrowing, until the fire died down, and then they heaped earth upon the spot where it had been, and placed his oar upon the mound as a memorial of their dead comrade, even as he had asked, so that he should not be forgotten.

They stayed one more night upon Aeaea. In the evening Circe came, followed by her serving-maids, bearing food and wine. Odysseus and his men sat upon the shore and ate and drank, telling Circe all that they had seen. And when night fell, they lay down to rest, but Circe led Odysseus aside and spoke with him.

'From Teiresias you have heard of perils that will beset you if you do not leave unharmed the cattle of the sun,' she said, 'but there are other dangers you may meet in sailing from these shores. Close by, upon a little isle, dwell the Sirens. They keep watch from the island, and sing to sailors rowing by. And of all the songs in the world, none is more beautiful than theirs, and whoever hears it forgets all else and would go to the Sirens on their isle. But all around them lie the bones of the men who have perished because of the spell cast by their singing. For on the island of the Sirens many men have languished, listening, till they died from want of food. Take care that you and your comrades do not hear the Sirens' song.

'Beyond this, two ways will lie open to you. One leads you by the Roaming Rocks, a high cliff against which the waves hurl themselves with so great a force that not even a bird might fly past, and no ship could make the journey. The other course lies along a narrow strait between two rocks, one tall and cloud-capped, the other low, with a great fig-tree growing upon it. Half-way up the tall rock there is a cave, and in this cave dwells Scylla, whose voice is as the yapping of a dog. She has twelve legs and six hideous heads on the ends of six long necks, and with each head she seizes one sailor from any ship that passes by. Beneath the other rock lurks Charybdis. Three times each day she sucks down the salt water into a foaming whirlpool, and three times each day she spouts it up, a seething fountain which engulfs all within its reach. If you would save your ship, Odysseus, sail close to Scylla's rock. It is better that six men should be lost than your whole company. And after that you will reach Thrinacia, where are herded the cattle of Helios, and against bringing hurt to these Teiresias warned you. To his sage words I add my entreaties. Sail clear of Thrinacia, Odysseus, if you and your companions wish to see your homes.'

Odysseus heeded well her words, and when she ceased, it was already dawn, and the golden sun was rising up above the water.

IV

Scylla and Charybdis and the Cattle of the Sun

THAT very day they set out once more on the long voyage home; and the enchantress Circe, who in the end had proved so good a friend to them, stood on the sand and watched the ship out of sight, speeded on its way by a fresh breeze which she herself had called up.

Once at sea, Odysseus thought fit to warn his men about the Sirens whose isle they soon would pass. But because he ever wished to know all that there was to know, he bade his comrades, when they neared the isle, bind him with strong ropes to the mast and resist all pleading to untie him; so that he might hear the song the Sirens sang. He took a round ball of beeswax, and cutting off pieces with his sword, he kneaded them with his fingers; until, warmed by the sunshine and his hands, the wax grew soft. Then with it he stopped the ears of all his men, so that they might hear nothing. Three of them then tied him to the mast with strong ropes, tightly knotted. A short distance on, the wind died down, and the men had to take to their oars; and thus they approached the Sirens' isle.

The two Sirens perched upon their little islet, which was like a flowery meadow whereon grew purple irises, many-hued anemones, and the little yellow crocus. But round the margin of the island, where the sea washed the shore, was a wide wreath of bones, whitened by the sun. The Sirens had the bodies of great feathered birds; wide wings and feet with claws; but their heads were as the heads of women, beautiful and kindly smiling, with long, flowing hair. And their voices were the sweetest sound in all the world.

'Come, brave Odysseus, noblest of the Greeks,' they sang, 'come to us and listen to our song. All men who go by our island pause to listen to our lay, and it gives them strength and courage and wisdom for all time. Only a madman or a fool would not stay for our singing, for we know and can sing of everything that has happened since the world began.'

When Odysseus heard their voices he forgot all else, and knew only that he must stay and listen to their song. And he signed to his men with nods and frowns to loose him from his bonds, and struggled to free himself; yet they took no notice of his signs, for he had bidden them heed him not. But when his struggles grew too violent, Eurylochus feared that the ropes might break, and jumping up, he went to Odysseus and tightened the bonds.

And when at last the ship had passed the Sirens and their singing could no longer be heard, Odysseus' men took the wax from their ears and unbound him.

But before he had time to answer their questions as to what song the Sirens sang and how sweet their voices were, a great noise was heard as of a mighty fountain, and Odysseus knew that they were near Charybdis. At once his men ceased rowing and stared before them in terror at the two rocks on either side of the narrow strait, one high and misty and the other low with a fig-tree growing on it.

Odysseus went among them with words of encouragement and comfort. 'My friends, we have been in many perils together, but we have lived through them all. And indeed, this new danger cannot be worse than the Cyclops in his cave; and yet I brought you out alive from that monster's den. Be guided by me now and we may be saved. Row as you have never rowed before, and look not aside from your oars.' Then to the helmsman he spoke, 'Steer clear of the churning and thundering around the lower of the rocks, and keep close in beside the tall cliff.' But he did not tell them of Scylla in her cave half-way up the rock, lest fear should take the strength from their arms and make them feeble.

In the hope that he might lop off one of Scylla's heads, Odysseus put on his helmet and took up his shield and sword and stood waiting on the deck, watching carefully the surface of the taller rock. It was indeed a high cliff, with its summit hidden in the mist, and its sides as smooth and polished as a silver mirror. But though he strained his eyes with looking, Odysseus could catch no sight of Scylla, nor hear her yapping like a little dog.

Opposite, no farther than a man could shoot an arrow, stood the low flat rock beneath which Charybdis dwelt. Upon it the great fig-tree stretched out its branches, thick with glossy leaves and green, unripe fruit. While below, when Charybdis sucked down the water, could be seen the very bottom of the sea; and when she spouted it forth again, it was like a great pot boiling over on a flaming fire, with spray and steam and swirling waters and a mighty hissing.

The nearer the ship came, the more awful grew the sound; and as they rowed into the narrow strait, Odysseus turned to see the foaming whirlpool and relaxed his watch for Scylla. Instantly she leant out from her cave half-way up the smooth rock and pounced upon a rower with each of her six heads. At their cries Odysseus turned, his sword ready, but it was even then too late and he could not reach the monster as she dangled the unhappy men above the ship. Her six hideous heads had each three rows of teeth, and struggle as they might, her poor victims could not escape; and she devoured them at the opening of her cave, while they yet called for help.

With all their might Odysseus' men rowed on, till at last they were safely past the rocks and out into the open sea.

But though they had won through the perils of Scylla and Charybdis with no more than the loss of six men, there lay before them that far greater danger of which both Teiresias and Circe had warned Odysseus: the cattle of the sun-god on the island of Thrinacia.

They sighted the island towards evening, and the thought of land was welcome indeed to the tired men. The first man to see it raised a shout, and all eyes looked eagerly to where he pointed. 'We are fortunate at last, and tonight we shall eat and sleep on land once more, away from the endless rolling of the sea.'

But even before they reached the island they heard the lowing of cattle and the bleating of sheep; and as they came nearer they could plainly see the herds and flocks grazing on the grassy meadows, fine beasts of mighty size and noble appearance, fit for the ownership of an immortal god, their sleek white hides and woolly fleeces gilded by the setting sun.

'It is the island of Thrinacia,' said Odysseus, 'and those beasts are the cattle and sheep of Helios, who is the sun. Both Teiresias the prophet and Circe the enchantress warned me with strict and earnest words that we should take care to harm not the herds of the sun if we would ever see our homes again. To avert the danger, let us not set foot upon the island. Row on, good men, and let us bear a small discomfort to avoid a greater grief.'

But they protested at his words, and called to him how tired they were, how weary of the sea; and reminded him that for hours they had been rowing, while he, their leader, had been idle, watching the blue water. He answered them without anger, for he knew they spoke the truth; but for all his compassion he would not let them land, but once more bade them row on; if need be, all through the night.

Then Eurylochus spoke bitterly. 'Because you are stronger than we are, Odysseus, and because your heart is iron, you will not grant us rest and the sweet relief of sleep upon a shore. Instead you order us to row on into the darkness, and who knows that we shall not be rowing on into a tempest which will wreck our ship and drown us every one, and all because you ordered it. Just for tonight let us cook our supper on the shore and sleep upon the sand, and in the morning we will sail with the first light of day.'

The men all called out in agreement. 'Yes, Odysseus, let us rest tonight. We will sail at dawn and no harm can come of it.'

So Odysseus sighed and gave way to their entreaties. But before they set foot upon the land, he made them swear an oath to keep from the sacred sheep and cattle on the isle, and be content with the provisions with which Circe had stocked their ship.

They moored the ship in a little harbour near a spring, and built fires upon the shore to cook their food, and unsealed a jar of rich crimson wine, made from the grapes of Aeaea. And when they had eaten and drunk, they lay down upon the sand and slept, wrapped in their warm cloaks.

But in the night a tempest rose and the wind blew wildly from the south, and in the morning it had not dropped and they could not sail. They dragged the ship up on to the beach and hid her in a cave; and once more Odysseus warned his men against harming the cattle which grazed peacefully in the pasture-lands so short a distance from the shore, and he gave orders that of the food which remained to them, no man was to have more than his fair daily share.

So long as there was food left they never questioned the wisdom of his warning; for there were none of them that doubted that it would be unwise to meddle with the property of an immortal god. But the south wind blew boisterously for a month, and long before the thirty days were over, the food was gone; and there was no wild game upon the island.

They drank cold water from the spring to calm their hunger; they dug up to eat, from deep below the sand, the bulbs of the sweet-scented white sea-lilies which grew above the water's edge; and searched among the rocks for crabs. With hooks of bent wire they fished, wading out from the shore; but rarely caught a fish of any size. They tore limpets from the rocks, and endlessly they turned over stones upon the beach, seeking for the little sea-creatures underneath. And once in a while a well-aimed stone would kill a sea-bird, and it would fall upon the shore. And ever in the ears of the starving men was the lowing of sleek cattle and the bleating of fat sheep; and ever before their eyes were the glossy white oxen and the snowy-fleeced sheep of Helios the sun-god.

When it was the twentieth day since they had landed on Thrinacia, while Odysseus, weakened by starvation, slept in a place that was sheltered from the ceaseless wind, Eurylochus spoke to his companions. 'Whatever way death comes to us, it comes unwelcomed, but I, at least, would prefer not to die of hunger. What say you, friends, why do we not drive off a few of the fattest of those cows and kill them while Odysseus sleeps? If the gods are angry with us afterwards, and wreck our ship, then no doubt we shall be drowned. But is it not better to die quickly in the sea, than slowly to starve with so much good meat grazing on every side?'

And because the men were hungry, and saw no other way to save their lives, they agreed with Eurylochus, and at once they went and drove off three or four of the finest of the cattle and killed and flayed them on the beach. They built a huge fire, and cutting up the meat, turned it on spits before the blaze; and never had they waited so longingly for a meal to cook.

Odysseus awoke to smell the roasting meat, and instantly he knew what had been done. With horror in his heart he ran back to the shore, and bitterly he blamed his men for their rash disobedience. But it was too late for help, and no one could undo the deed. The sacred cattle had been killed and cooked, and such a crime it was certain Helios would never overlook.

'The immortal gods will avenge this sacrilege,' said Odysseus, 'there will be no escape for us.'

And truly, in that moment the anger of the gods was shown in wondrous signs. A lowing as of cattle came from the meat upon the spits, and the flayed hides moved upon the sands. But for all these portents Odysseus' men could not hold back from the meat, but fell upon it and ate eagerly.

For six days longer they remained on Thrinacia, and on the seventh day the wind dropped and veered, and at once they dragged the ship down to the water's edge, and unfurling the sail, put out to sea, leaving behind them the island where they had spent so many bitter days, and the herds which were soon to bring disaster on them.

When the island was out of sight, and no other land had appeared on the horizon, a black cloud moved across the sun and a heavy shadow lay over the sea and a wild wind came howling from the west. The wind broke the forestays of the mast, so that the mast fell into the ship, killing the helmsman as it fell. A flash of lightning struck the ship asunder, and Odysseus' men were hurled into the waves; and not one of them was saved.

But Odysseus clung on to the wrecked ship until the sea battered her apart, breaking away the sides and tearing off the mast by the keel. Then lashing the keel and the mast together with the ox-hide backstay, Odysseus held to them, driven over the waves by the rushing wind.

After a time the west wind died down, and the south wind arose, blowing Odysseus back across the sea towards the straits where dwelt Scylla and Charybdis.

At dawn, he saw that he was close by the vortex of Charybdis, and try as he might with all his strength, he could not keep the mast and keel from being sucked down by the hidden monster.

As they vanished into the whirlpool, Odysseus jumped clear and clutched hold of the trunk of the fig-tree growing from the rock. He held on to it with hands and legs, unable to climb up into the branches for they hung too high above his head, and unable to gain a firmer foothold for the rock was too low down. There he clung, like a bat upon a wall, until Charybdis spouted forth the mast and keel. Then he let himself drop back into the water, and clambering once more upon these precious spars, rowed with his hands in frantic haste, away from the dread rock where Charybdis lurked, before she should gulp down another draught of sea.

And after that, for nine days Odysseus clung to the mast and keel, borne here and there across the sea, and on the tenth day he was washed ashore on the island of Ogygia.

V

Calypso

ON the island of Ogygia lived the nymph Calypso, immortal and ever young, with unchanging beauty. She dwelt in a wide grotto set within a grove of trees; dark cypresses, alders, and the rustling poplar, which made a shelter for the cavern from the rough winds of the sea.

Before the entrance to her home grew many flowers; white, pink, and mauve anemones, the ivory spears of crocuses which opened to the sun, resin-scented rock-roses; and under the shade of the tall trees, little violets and bright blue squills. From four clear springs flowed water, cool and pure as crystal; while around each fountain flourished those plants which love damp soil, the sweet-scented, fragile, dark purple iris and the fragrant flowering rush. The grove was the home of many birds, swift hawks and harsh-voiced crows, and the owl which calls by night. Around the entrance to the grotto, its leaves fringing the opening, climbed a huge vine, where, all seasons alike, hung heavy bunches of ripe purple grapes.

Within, the cave itself was richly furnished and divided into rooms. The rocky walls were hung with patterned cloths, and green reeds and sweet herbs were strewn upon the floor. The chairs and tables were of cunningly carved wood; and set in a place where it caught the greatest light stood Calypso's loom, with a golden shuttle, whereon she wove the everlasting cloth which would not perish with the years.

The nymph Calypso, walking on the shore, found Odysseus lying on the sand, half-drowned, starving, and exhausted. She took him to her grotto and brought him back to life and health by virtue of her magic drugs. And as the days passed and he grew strong again, she came to love him, and offered him immortality and everlasting youth if he would only stay with her upon her island. But Odysseus was homesick for Ithaca, and he grieved for his wife and little son, and longed to see them both again; so with courtesy he refused her gifts. But for all that, Calypso would not let him leave her, and kept him with her on Ogygia for seven years.

In spite of the company of an immortal nymph and the ease and comfort of his life in the grotto, and in spite of the fair island and its many delights, Odysseus pined and mourned continually, sitting on the shore and looking ever out to sea, remembering that beyond the blue waters, somewhere, lay his home.

From the cloud-crowned heights of Mount Olympus, home of the immortal gods, the wise goddess Athene looked down upon the sufferings of Odysseus and pitied him. He was a man whose life she had watched with approval, for his wiles and his resourcefulness had given her much pleasure.

Blue-eyed and sternly beautiful, white-robed and with a helmet of everlasting gold, she stood up in the council of the immortal gods and spoke. 'Father Zeus and all you other ever-living gods, what profit shall a man have who lives in virtue, righteousness, and justice, ruling his people kindly and with ever an eye to good, if we, who ordain all things, take no care to reward him for his ways? Truly, it would be more to a man's advantage to oppress and steal, and to kill all those whom he rules over, if we, the immortal gods, send misfortunes to the good and bad alike. There was a king in Ithaca, Odysseus was he named, no prince ever ruled more kindly, and his people loved him with all their hearts. With many other leaders of the Greeks he left his home and family and sailed to fight at Troy. When the city was taken he set out for Ithaca once more, but ill fortune sailed with him. His ships were lost, his men were drowned, and he himself, after many perils passed, found safety on an island where the nymph Calypso dwelt. There for seven years he languished, longing for his home, a prisoner to her love for him. No ship had he in which to sail away, no skill to fight against the powers of the immortal nymph, no strength to break free from her toils.

Father Zeus and all you other ever-living gods, you all do know Odysseus, his virtue, his brave deeds, his courage. Judge you then he has deserved the misfortunes you have heaped on him?'

From his high throne, Zeus, father of gods and men, answered her, 'My daughter, we have not forgotten wise Odysseus, his virtue, his brave deeds, his courage. Nor do we think him to deserve the misfortunes you have told us of. Indeed, those misfortunes did not come from us, but from our brother, Poseidon, lord of all the seas. For he was angered when Odysseus blinded his son, Polyphemus the Cyclops, and since that day has he pursued Odysseus with his wrath, and brought to nothing all his struggles to see his home once more. It is from Poseidon, and from him alone, that all Odysseus' troubles come.'

Quickly Athene spoke again. 'Father Zeus, now let it be your will to free Odysseus from his durance on the island of Ogygia. If it is pleasing to you, send Hermes, our messenger, to bid the nymph Calypso release her prisoner.'

Zeus smiled a little. 'So let it be, my daughter.' And he called to Hermes the messenger to come to him, and said, 'Go, Hermes, and carry to Calypso our command, that she release Odysseus from her toils, so that he may once more see his home. But since it is fated that he shall return to Ithaca alone, after much suffering and by his own labours, then for him to leave Ogygia shall there be no ship, but only a raft built by his own hands. Go, my son, and tell this to Calypso.'

At once Hermes bound on his winged sandals, the gift of Zeus himself, which could carry him over the land and sea more swiftly than the wind; and taking his wand, with

the lightest touch of which he could give to mortals sleep or waking at his will, he stepped down from Olympus, home of the immortal gods, and sped across the sea to the island of Ogygia, skimming over the waves like a bird.

On the island, Odysseus sat upon the shore and sighed, looking out to sea, and Calypso was alone within her grotto, weaving. She wore a silvery robe that gleamed like moonlight, with a golden girdle round her waist; and over her bright hair, a veil as fine as gossamer. She moved before her loom, weaving the everlasting cloth from many-coloured magic threads, and under her nimble fingers the golden shuttle sped to and fro, faster than the eye could watch. And as she worked, she sang.

Hermes called to her from the entrance to the cavern, where he stood beneath the trailing vine. 'Greetings, fair Calypso.'

She turned and saw him there, and at once she knew him for the immortal messenger. For though they may deceive a mortal man, the gods and divine beings cannot hide themselves from one another, and whatever shape they choose to take, at once they recognize each other. She dropped her golden shuttle. 'Greetings, swift Hermes, you are welcome to my home.'

She led him in and set two chairs beside the blazing fire of scented cedar logs which filled the grotto with its fragrance. She placed between them a table with ambrosia on a golden dish and nectar in two crystal cups; and together they sat and ate ambrosia, food of the gods alone, and drank the rosy nectar which might pass only immortal lips.

And when they had eaten and drunk, she asked him,

'Tell me, Hermes, why have you come here today, across the wide stretch of barren sea that separates our homes? It is not often that I, living on this lonely island, entertain a guest from Mount Olympus. I must confess, I am curious to learn the reason for your visit.'

Hermes laughed. 'It is, as you have said, fair Calypso, a wide stretch of sea that separates our homes, and not willingly would one fly across that endless, tedious waste of blue. But it was Zeus who sent me, else should I not be here, despite the pleasure that it gives me to speak with you again.'

'And what message has Father Zeus for me?'

'He says that here upon your island there is a man, unhappiest of all the Greeks who fought at Troy, Odysseus, king of Ithaca. Here in your company he pines, and longs to see his home. It is the will of Father Zeus that you now release this man with speed, that he may return to Ithaca.'

For a long time Calypso did not speak, and then her voice was bitter. 'You are cruel and jealous, you gods who live far off upon Olympus. You envy me my happiness and would take it from me. I found Odysseus dying on the beach, washed upon my island shores by the heartless waves. I brought him to my grotto, I tended him and fed him, and with my healing drugs I gave him back his life. As we immortals may grant to whom we please the power to live for ever, so would I have given to Odysseus everlasting youth and eternal happiness here with me. But he would not take the gifts I offered in affection, for he still frets for a rocky island where once he had a home, and dreams of a woman who, I doubt not, for all she is a mortal, was fair enough, some seventeen years ago. But I had hope that one day he would forget his kingdom, that one day I might blot out utterly from his mind all remembrance of his wife. And I had no doubt but that in the end I should prevail, and we two should dwell here in happiness for ever. And now with your words you have torn away my hope.'

'The words, divine Calypso, came from Zeus, whom all gods and mortals must obey.'

'I had no thought but to obey. Odysseus may leave me when he will. It is the command of Zeus.' Calypso rose. 'But Zeus must see him safely back to Ithaca. I keep no ships upon the island for sending shipwrecked sailors home. It is enough that I let him go.'

'Be not too angered at the will of Zeus,' said Hermes gently, 'and give Odysseus what good counsel you can as to how he may reach home. For I know you would not have him perish on the ever-hungry sea.'

After a while Calypso smiled. 'I will give him all the good counsel that I can, for he is very dear to me,' she said quietly. 'Farewell, Hermes.'

Calypso went to Odysseus where he sat upon the shore, crouched on a rock with his head hidden in his hands. She touched his shoulder and spoke to him. 'Look up, Odysseus, and cease your sorrowing, for the seven years you have found so long and weary will soon be ended, and with my blessing and a fair wind to speed you, you will be sailing for your home.'

Odysseus looked at her. 'I have no ship,' he said. 'How can I sail to my own home, or to anywhere else in the world?'

'I will give you an axe,' she said, 'that with it you may cut wood and build yourself a raft, firm and stout to resist the waves, with a tall mast and a sail. And I will give you clothes to keep you warm, and food and wine for the voyage, and call up the wind to carry you swiftly home.'

But staring at the sand Odysseus thought well upon her words, for they brought no comfort to his heart, but only deep unease.

'Why are you silent?' she asked him. 'I had thought you would be glad to know that you were to see your home once more.'

He turned his head to her and spoke out his mind. 'Not even all the well-built ships that sail upon the sea reach safely home to port. How then shall a little raft, manned by me alone, survive the violence of the wind and the fury of the waves? No, immortal lady, I will not trust myself to the merciless sea and the sweeping tempests of the sky in a raft of my own making, though you induce me, for I fear you persuade me to my hurt.'

Calypso took his hands in hers and smiled at him. 'Odysseus,' she said, 'when will you learn that I love you well, and would protect you from all harm?'

'When you have sworn an oath that in this thing you mean no ill to me.'

'You are ever cautious and ever prudent, Odysseus. To please you I will swear an oath as you desire, an oath that would bind even an immortal god, and then perchance you will be satisfied.'

And when she had sworn he trusted her words, and considered with more favour the building of a raft, on which to sail for Ithaca.

Together they returned to the grotto and ate and drank their evening meal. As they sat beside the fragrant, smouldering cedar logs, Odysseus thought about the raft for his journey home, and in his mind he planned its making, rejecting one idea and approving another. As he leant forward, looking into the fire and seeing it not, his eyes were bright and on his face there was a look of eagerness which Calypso had not seen there before.

She laughed a little. 'Are you so impatient to be gone from me, Odysseus? Are you so wearied of my love for you that even in my company you sit silent, dreaming of your wife? Is she so fair, Odysseus? Surely no mortal woman could be more beautiful than I.'

Odysseus looked at her and shook his head. 'Do not be angry with my words,' he said quietly. 'Though I know well no mortal woman could compare with you in beauty, nor is it fitting that she should, yet to me my wife Penelope is fair enough. And that enough is more than all the immortality and ageless youth you offer me.'

'The choice is yours,' she said. 'But if you could guess the perils that wait for you before your journey will be ended, you might choose to remain here with me and take my gifts. And because I am no mortal, talking idly in the dark, and because to me it is given to read the future when I wish, my words are not the foolish babbling of a weak, fond woman trying to persuade you against your will.'

'Divine Calypso, I know you speak the truth, and for my good. But though I knew that I should almost surely perish on the sea, even so could I not hold back from this voyage, but would take still the chance that you offer me to see once more my home and family.'

And to his words she gave no reply, marvelling in silence at the strange ways of mortal men.

The next morning Calypso gave Odysseus a sharp axe of bronze and an auger for drilling holes, and he set off for the farthest shore of the little island, where the trees grew tall and straight. Here beneath the pines bloomed yellow crocuses and dark wine-red anemones, and from the branches the thrushes sang. Odysseus' heart was light as he went among the trees, choosing out those most fitted to his needs.

When he had chosen twenty trees, he set to work to fell them. That done, he lopped off all the branches and fashioned fifteen of the trunks into smooth poles of equal length. Drilling each pole at each end with the auger, he fastened them firmly together with wooden pegs, forming a level platform as wide as the hull of a merchant's ship.

From the five tree trunks that remained, he put by two straight firs, one for the mast and the other, slightly shorter, for the yard. The other three he split and hewed into planks which he laid athwartships across the platform to form the deck. Then he set up stanchions along each side, pegging the bulwarks to them; so making a strong wall against the waves, and finishing with a specially stout plank along the top to form the gunwale. As a final protection he enclosed each of the four sides with a wickerwork of plaited withies.

Across the bow of his raft he set up a thwart with an opening above a mast-step. And when he had made the mast smooth and round and drilled a hole from one side of it to the other, through which to reeve the halyard, he lowered it through the opening in the thwart and wedged it firmly into the step. Then at the stern he mounted an oar for steering.

Calypso brought him sailcloth, woven by her own hands; and while she watched him, he cut it skilfully, sewed it to the bolt rope and bent it to the yard. Lastly he braided strong ropes from thongs and pliant osiers; shrouds to stay the mast, a halyard for hoisting the yard, braces for trimming it to the wind, and sheets to hold the clews of the sail.

The raft was finished, and, with logs for launching ways, he brought her to the water's edge. Then at last his work was done, and it had taken him but four days, so eagerly had he laboured.

Odysseus spent one final night in Calypso's grotto, and in the morning he took to the raft the skins of wine and water she had given him, a leathern bag of food, enough to last him many days, and warm raiment to protect him from the cold.

She came down to the shore with him, and watched him stow away her gifts. 'Sail always with the Great Bear on your left,' she told him, 'and you will at length reach the land of Phaeacia.'

'I will remember,' he said. 'Immortal lady, my thanks are but a poor offering to you, but they are all I have to give. Take them and wish me well.'

'Thank me not, Odysseus, for were it not the will of Father Zeus, whom all gods and mortals must obey, my heart would be lighter at this moment, and,' she smiled, 'yours, I think, more heavy. Now go, for I wish you well, but I would not have you see an immortal grieve.'

Then bidding her farewell, he unfurled his sail, and blown on his way by the warm breeze she called up for him, he set off across the wide sea.

For seventeen days he sailed with a gentle wind and a clear sky, ever with the Great Bear on his left, and on the eighteenth day he sighted land. Overjoyed, he steered his raft towards the misty outline of the distant cliffs.

Yet his joy lasted but a little time, for Poseidon, god of the seas, saw him as he sailed, and remembering his implacable vengeance, he called the clouds together and stirred up the sea, drove forth the winds over the water, and hastened the night. The four winds flung themselves upon the sea and lifted up a mighty wave and bore it down upon the raft.

Odysseus saw it coming and clung to the steering oar. 'This', he thought, 'will surely be the end of my voyaging for ever. Better would it have been had I died before the walls of Troy, as did so many of the Greeks. There at least should I not have lacked friends to mourn me, and comrades to carry home the tidings of my death. But now shall I perish far from the sight of men, and no word of my ending shall ever reach to Ithaca.'

The great wave struck the raft, snatching the steering-oar from Odysseus' grasp, and sweeping him into the dark sea, snapping the mast in two and carrying away the yard. Weighed down by the heavy clothes Calypso had given him to protect him from cold winds, Odysseus struggled to climb back on to the raft. Once on her, he flung himself down upon the deck-planks, holding fast to one of her sides, while the winds chased her to and fro across the ocean, as though they played a game.

He would assuredly have been destroyed had not Ino, the sea-nymph, seen him, and because she herself had once been a mortal, she pitied him. In her life on earth she had been a queen, and fleeing from death had leapt into the sea, and the gods had given her everlasting life and magic powers. Remembering now her long-past misfortunes, she came to help Odysseus, flashing up through the wild sea and standing beside him on the raft, with her limbs like pale ivory in the darkness and the wind whipping through her long, wet hair.

Her voice was like the murmur that is heard inside a shell, yet he heard it clearly above the storm. 'Unhappy Odysseus, to have aroused the anger of Poseidon, ruler of the seas. But do not despair, for indeed he shall not slay you and your life is not yet done. Do but what I bid you and you will be saved. Strip off your clothes that you may swim the better, and leaving your raft to be blown by the winds, make for the coast that lies before you. I will give you my veil, for it holds a strong enchantment, and he who wears it cannot drown. But when you have reached the shore, then, with your eyes turned away toward the land, cast it back into the sea. Here, take the veil, wind it about your waist, and plunge into the waves.'

He took the filmy scarf she handed him, and when he looked again, she had gone, as silently and swiftly as a bird of the sea, and he was alone in the darkness. And if it had not been for the veil in his hands, he would have thought she never had been there.

It was not Odysseus' way to trust easily the words of others, and he thought carefully of Ino's advice. 'What if it should be', he said to himself, 'that one of the immortal gods has set a trap for me? Perchance the divine nymph was sent by Poseidon to tempt me to leave the raft, the only protection left to me from the all-engulfing sea. No,

I will rather remain here until my raft is torn asunder by the waves, then will it be time enough to swim.'

But even while he was thinking thus, a great wave curved over the raft and crashed down upon it, breaking the boards apart and scattering wood across the sea. Washed into the water, Odysseus clung to a plank, and clambering up to sit astride it, he flung off the garments Calypso had given him, and wound Ino's magic veil around his waist, knotting it securely. Then he dived into the water and swam in the direction of the coast.

For two days and two nights he was in the sea, sometimes striving against the waves, and sometimes drifting with them; but on the dawn of the third day the wind dropped and the sea grew calm, and Odysseus saw that he was close in to the shore. Eagerly he swam on, his weary body winning strength from the welcome sight to make one final effort.

But as he came nearer to the coast, he heard the sea thundering on the reefs, and knew that here were no gently sloping beaches where a tired swimmer might walk ashore; but only sharp rocks and craggy cliffs, and the surf battering against them.

'What now shall I do?' he wondered. 'Weary as I am, I yet dare go no farther in, for I should be torn to pieces on the pitiless rocks.'

At that moment he was seized by a huge breaker which carried him forwards towards the shore, and he would indeed have been killed upon the reef had he not grasped hold of a rock as he was swept along. There he clung while the wave rushed past him, but as it flowed backward again, he was torn from the rock and washed out to sea. With all his might he battled against the incoming waves until he reached the calm water beyond the breakers, and, keeping an eye ever towards the shore for the sight of a shelving beach where he might land, he swam farther along the coast.

Just when it seemed to him as though he could surely go no longer, but must choose between drowning in the deep sea or being dashed to pieces on the crags in a last attempt to land, he caught sight of the mouth of a river, where it flowed into the ocean.

Joyfully he swam to it, and a little way upstream, where the sand and stones sloped gently to the river's edge, he came ashore. On the ground he lay, weak and exhausted, with no longer the strength to move. But when he was a little recovered, the first thing that he did was to unwind from his body the magic veil, and with eyes averted, he dropped it into the river, and the stream bore it out to sea and across the waves to Ino.

Then Odysseus thought, 'Weary as I am, I cannot lie here, for when darkness falls and the chill night comes, then shall I likely die of cold, so weak am I after my torments in the sea.'

And he stumbled a little way farther up the river's bank, to where there was a small wood beside the stream, with a fair meadow beyond, running down to the water's edge. Here in this thicket he found two bushes growing near together, an olive and a wild olive, their branches close entwined to form a shelter from the wind, and their grey-green leaves thickly spread against the rain and sun. Under these bushes, on a heap of dried leaves, Odysseus lay down, covering himself with the dead, rustling foliage, and in this soft, warm bed he fell asleep.

VI

Nausicaa

IN the night before the morning when Odysseus reached Phaeacia, swimming up the river's mouth to safety, in the palace of Alcinous, king of that land, his young daughter, Nausicaa, had a dream.

Nausicaa was a lovely maiden with a happy smile, and not long since, she had been no more than a child. But now she had reached an age at which a maiden begins to think of marriage, and King Alcinous was watching carefully the young Phaeacian noblemen, that he might choose a husband wisely for his daughter.

In her dream Nausicaa saw a friend of hers, a maiden her own age, who said to her, 'Nausicaa, why do you lie abed so lazily? Soon the day will come when you will be wedded to a husband of your father's choice; not much longer will you remain unmarried. Few things are more fitting for a young bride than that she should have a bounteous store of fair, clean garments to carry with her, folded in chests of carved or painted wood, to her husband's house. And what of the maidens who will follow you, singing the marriage songs? And your brothers who will dance and rejoice in the palace on your wedding-day? Is it meet they should not have fine clothes to wear? Come, Nausicaa, you are a princess and the daughter of a king, only the best in all things is good enough for you. It is a shame that there should be so many fine garments lying crumpled and unwashed about the house. Gather them together and take them to the river that they may be clean and smoothly folded for your marriage-day.'

When Nausicaa awoke in the morning, she remembered her dream, and thought the advice she had been given was good. So she went to her father and said to him, 'Dear father, may I take a wagon down to the river today with all our clothes that are lying in the store-rooms waiting to be washed? For you are the king and it is right that you should have a plentiful supply of fresh, clean clothes to wear at banquets and in the assembly place. And besides, I have five brothers, they are always wanting new, gay attire to wear for dancing.'

But because she was shy to speak to him of her own marriage, she said no word of that; yet King Alcinous understood and was glad that his daughter should take thought to have all things arranged fittingly for her wedding-day, when it should come; and he replied, 'You may have a wagon or anything else you want, my child. I will bid the servants make it ready for you, with two of the best mules to draw it, so that you may set out for the river at once.'

So while Nausicaa and her serving-maids gathered together the garments, the mules were yoked to the wagon; and by the time they carried out the bundles of clothes, white, with gay embroidery or woven patterns, or purple-dyed, or blue, the wagon was waiting before the porch. The clothes were piled into the cart and Nausicaa's mother, Arete the queen, saw that she had a basket of food and a jar of wine to take with her. Then Nausicaa climbed into the wagon and took up the reins and the mules trotted off through the streets of the city and into the country beyond at a good pace; but not too fast, for the serving-maids were walking behind the cart, chattering gaily.

On they went, past fields where the first green shoots of the corn showed above the earth; past hedges with straggling little almond trees whose blossoms, once white and rose and fresh, had faded to a greyish-pink among their opening leaf-buds as the year advanced.

When they reached the river close by the sea, they tumbled the clothes out on to the grass, and unyoking the mules from the wagon, tethered them where they might graze. Then Nausicaa and her maids tucked up their tunics to their knees and flinging the garments in the water, one by one, they trod them in the shallow basins by the river's edge, where the water flowed clear and pure above the flat stones. When all the clothes were washed, they wrung them out, then shook them and smoothed away the creases and laid them on the clean pebbles of the sea-shore to dry in the hot sun.

Then Nausicaa and her handmaidens took off their tunics,

and pinning up their hair carefully on the tops of their heads, they themselves went into the stream to bathe. Cooled and refreshed, they dried themselves upon the river bank, and putting on their tunics once again, they let down and combed their hair. The sun had by this time reached the highest point in its journey through the sky, so they chose a shady spot under a willow-tree, and unpacking the basket of food and opening the jar of wine, they sat down to eat their meal among the sweet-scented, many-flowered narcissi growing on the bank. They ate and drank and talked, and then for a time they sat quietly, idly plucking stems of the gold-cupped white narcissi to adorn themselves, while they waited for the clothes to dry.

At length one of the serving-maids said to Nausicaa, 'Mistress, may we not play a game? For the sun is less high now, and it will not be so hot.'

Nausicaa jumped up. 'Come,' she said, 'let us play. Did one of you think to bring a ball?'

The maid who had spoken ran to fetch her ball from the wagon; and when they had chosen out by lot one of their number, the others stood around her in a ring and tossed the ball over her head from one to another. The maiden in the centre tried to catch the ball as it passed her, and when she was successful she changed places with the thrower. While they played they sang, and Nausicaa, whose voice was the sweetest there, led them in the song.

For many minutes they enjoyed their game, until, the tallest of the handmaidens being in the centre, Nausicaa, trying to throw the ball too high for her to catch, sent it soaring up beyond the reach of the maid for whom it had been intended, and it fell into the river with a splash.

'Oh, my ball!' cried one of the maidens, running to the bank. 'Oh, mistress, you have thrown it into the river.'

The other maids ran after her, crying out and calling to each other. 'We shall never get it back, it is much too far out in the water. The river is deep in the middle, shall one of us swim out and get it back?'

Their excited cries awoke Odysseus, asleep under the olive-trees a short distance off, and he crept to the edge of the thicket to see what manner of people they were whose voices had disturbed him. When he saw the group of maidens clustered by the river he felt great relief. 'They look gentle and kindly', he thought, 'and doubtless will take pity on a poor shipwrecked wanderer. Naked and battered by the waves, I am no fit sight for strangers, but food and clothes I must have, and I shall throw myself on the mercy of these maidens.' So he came forth from among the trees and went towards them.

One of the serving-maids saw him and screamed. The others looked where she pointed and with cries fled in all directions. All save Nausicaa. And because she was a princess, and the daughter of a king, though no whit less afraid than they, she did not run away; but instead she stood there, between the river and Odysseus, in her white robe, with her heart beating very fast and her eyes open very wide, and a spray of narcissus in her hair.

Coming towards her, Odysseus wondered whether he should go to kneel at her feet, or whether she would be offended if he approached so close; and then he saw that she was very young and not a little afraid. So standing where he was he spoke to her with carefully chosen words; saying, though he knew well she was a mortal maiden,

'Noble lady, I know not whether you are one of the immortal goddesses, or some fair nymph whose home is by this river, for indeed you seem to me to be much like a goddess. But if you are a mortal maiden, then happy indeed are your parents to have so gracious a daughter, and fortunate are they who call you sister, yet most blessed of all will be he who will one day be your husband. But goddess, nymph, or mortal maiden, I here implore your pity for an unhappy wretch, cast upon your shore after twenty days of tossing on the sea. Who lives in this country I know not, but on your mercy I throw myself, pleading for some ragged piece of cloth that may serve me for a garment, and for word of how I may soonest reach a town.'

Nausicaa smiled a little, and felt much less afraid, now that she found the stranger was in distress and to be pitied. 'This is the land of Phaeacia,' she replied, 'whose king is Alcinous. I am his daughter, and I can promise you that the Phaeacians will treat you kindly, for they are friendly people.' And she called to her serving-maids, bidding them come back and leave their hiding-places, and scolding them for flying from a helpless wanderer. 'Come, see if there is food and wine left that he may eat, and I myself will pick out for him a tunic and a cloak from among the drying clothes.'

And while Odysseus bathed in the river, washing off the salt sea brine from his body, the maids spread out for him the bread and wine and little barley cakes left over from their meal; and Nausicaa chose for him a warm woollen cloak and a tunic of white linen with a woven border in a design of purple grapes, made by her mother, Queen Arete.

As he sat and ate the food, Nausicaa and her handmaidens folded the dry garments and packed them in the wagon, whispering together with many glances towards him. 'Indeed,' said Nausicaa, 'now that he is bathed and clothed the stranger seems to me to be a goodly man. Perhaps he may remain among us and make Phaeacia his home. Truly, when the day comes when I must marry, I wish that such a man as he might be my husband.'

When the clothes were laid away, Nausicaa bade her maids harness the mules to the cart, and going to Odysseus said, 'Stranger, we are now returning to my father's house, for the sun will soon be setting. If you will come with us, I will direct you to the city. While we are on the track that runs through the fields, until we reach the road that leads into the town, follow the wagon with my maids; but outside the city walls there stands a poplar grove, here would I ask you to wait a little space alone, before entering the city and asking for my father's house.' She blushed a little and went on, 'For if I, their princess, were seen in the streets in the company of a stranger, people might talk of it, and gossip, and say that I think myself too fine to wander in the country with my own fellow townsmen, but am ready enough to bid a stranger pass the time with me.'

'You are wise, princess,' Odysseus said with courtesy, 'and I commend your prudence. I will do as you bid me, and wait in the grove until such time as I think you will have reached your father's house.'

'You will find my home easily,' said Nausicaa. 'Ask anyone in the city where lies the palace of King Alcinous, and he will point it out to you. Even a child could tell you where it stands. Pass straight through the courtyard into the great hall and go at once to my mother, Arete, the queen, who usually sits spinning by the hearth. For my father respects her words and judgement, and if she gives you her protection, all will be well for you.'

With that Nausicaa climbed into the cart and urged the mules homewards; while Odysseus with the serving-maids walked behind along the roadway.

At sunset, outside the city walls, as she had said, they came to a grove of poplar trees. Here Nausicaa left Odysseus, going on with her maids alone. He waited in the pleasant grove until he judged she should be home, and then he walked on up to the city walls and passed through the tall gates.

The city had been built on an incurving stretch of coastline, so that it had a sheltered harbour lying on either side, with many ships drawn up to the quay, their rigging black against the gold and yellow sunset. Because the Phaeacians were a sea-loving people, they had built their assembly place close by the harbour; stone benches in a semicircle, and a fine stretch of sandy ground before, for games or dancing.

Odysseus was directed to the palace by a little girl, and found it a lofty building surrounded by wide gardens and a hedged-in orchard with orderly rows of apples, pears, pomegranates, figs, and olives. Close by there was a vineyard, and beds of herbs for cooking, spices and aromatic plants for flavouring the dishes. In these grounds there were two springs, one which flowed through the gardens and the other which ran to a fountain at the great gates of the palace, where the townspeople came to fill their pitchers.

Odysseus crossed the courtyard and stood on the threshold of the palace, marvelling at all he saw. The doors were golden, with door-posts of silver, and the threshold itself was of bronze. On either side of the door stood a dog fashioned of silver, the fierce-looking guardians of the palace. Odysseus passed through the door and crossed the pillared vestibule to the door of the great hall. Inside the hall was even more magnificence. The walls were bronze with a frieze of blue, and all along them ran seats with bright-coloured woven covers and soft cushions, and raised above the seats, on pedestals, stood golden statues, lovely youths holding torches which flared to light the feasting in the hall.

Odysseus saw King Alcinous sitting on his high throne among his friends and counsellors, and close beside the fire, not too far off from the king, he saw a stately grey-haired woman spinning. 'That will be the queen, whom the princess bade me ask for help,' he thought. And going forward boldly he knelt before her.

'Greetings, Queen Arete, and long life and happiness to you. I ask your pity for a stranger, far from his home, and beg that with your help he may once again see his own land, across the wide sea.' And Odysseus sat down in the hearth among the ashes and waited to see what the Phaeacians would do.

For a time they were all silent in surprise, and then an elder of the council, a much-respected nobleman, spoke. 'It is not fitting, King Alcinous, that a stranger should sit among the ashes in your hall, while we are feasting here.'

The king looked towards the queen, and when she smiled

in agreement, he rose, and going to Odysseus held out his hand to him. 'You are welcome, stranger,' he said, 'come and sit and eat with us.' And he led Odysseus to a seat next to his throne, where his favourite son, Laodamas, was wont to sit, and the young man rose with a smile and gave Odysseus his chair.

The servants brought him food and drink, and he feasted with his kind hosts well into the night; and when at last the other guests rose to go, King Alcinous said, 'My friends, we have among us today a stranger, and very welcome he is to our fair city. In the morning let us all meet at the assembly place, and there devise some means of entertainment for him, before we send him home across the sea, that in the years to come, when he is happy in his own land, he may remember Phaeacia with kindness.'

To this they all assented, and one by one they bade the king and his family good night and went. Then, too, the king's five sons all went to their rest, and Alcinous, Queen Arete, and Odysseus were left alone in the great hall, while the servants moved quietly about, clearing away the tables and the dishes.

Alcinous drew two chairs up by the fire, close to where his wife was sitting, and the three of them sat together silently, each thinking his own thoughts.

Arete was the first to speak. She had been waiting until the guests were gone to ask her question, for from the moment he had knelt at her feet, she had recognized the tunic Odysseus was wearing, for she had woven it herself. 'Stranger,' she said, 'who are you, and where is your home? Did you not say that you came from across the sea?

Tell me, from whom did you receive this tunic that you wear?'

'Most gracious queen, after seven years' captivity on the island of Ogygia, where dwells the nymph Calypso, I put out to sea on a raft which I myself had made. Upon this raft for seventeen days I sailed. But on the eighteenth day a wild storm broke, my raft was wrecked, and I myself, after two days and nights tossed upon the waves, was cast upon your shores, close by a river. Here, as I slept, I was awakened by the sound of voices. It was your daughter and her handmaidens. From her I begged a garment to clothe myself, and she gave me this cloak and tunic from among those which she had drying on the shore. And when I asked her to direct me to the city, she brought me with her as far as the fair grove which lies beyond your city walls. And there she left me to come on alone and make my way to your palace, where she promised me I should find a welcome.'

'She spoke truly,' said Arete. 'You are indeed most welcome, stranger.'

But Alcinous said, 'I must beg you to forgive her. She is very young, and young maidens are often foolish. She should not have left you at the grove, she should have brought you home with her and told me how she found you, and thus you would have been spared coming alone into a strange house to ask a favour.'

Odysseus spoke quickly. 'You must not blame her, King Alcinous, she did all she might for me, and indeed she bade me come with her to the palace to speak with you. But I would not, and waited rather in the grove, that I might come after, alone. For I had no way of knowing what manner of man you were, and sometimes we men are jealous when we see a stranger thrusting himself into our families and wheedling his way into the good graces or our womenfolk.'

This kindly lie Alcinous at once believed, and he was pleased to think both that the stranger was a man of such good sense, and that his young daughter had not shown herself so forgetful of the duties of hospitality as to leave a stranger in misfortune to find his way to her home alone. He laughed. 'As I hope you will have seen by now, I am not a man like that. I believe that tempers are best kept, and that all things and all men deserve to be judged on their own merits, and not by any common standard. And I well believe that you are of like mind, such a man as I would willingly see my daughter wedded to, should you desire to remain in this country, an honoured member of my family, with a goodly house and such possessions as I would gladly give you.'

For a moment Odysseus hesitated, wondering what best to say that would not make a refusal of such a kindly offer seem ungracious. But Alcinous noticed the hesitation and went on at once, 'Or if you should prefer to return to your own land, then willingly shall I have made ready for you one of our fine ships, with as many of our young men as may row her most swiftly to your home. For we here in Phaeacia love the sea, and there is no other land whose people are so skilled at managing a tall ship as are our men, who learn to know the sea from the time they are but children.'

Odysseus thanked him, his heart full with gratitude, that at last he saw near the end of his wandering. 'May you be rewarded for your kindness, good Alcinous,' he said.

That night, for the first time since he had left Ogygia on his raft, Odysseus slept in a comfortable bed with a woollen coverlet and purple-dyed blankets, in the vestibule beyond the great hall, where it was the custom for all guests to sleep.

VII

King Alcinous and the Phaeacians

IN the morning the Phaeacians gathered in the assembly place, beside the harbour, and to them came King Alcinous, with Odysseus at his side. He told his people once again about the stranger who had reached their shores, and of his promise to send him safely home. 'Go,' he said, 'pick out two-and-fifty of our finest sailors and let them make ready the swiftest ship we have, so that our unknown guest may with all speed be carried to his home.'

Quickly they obeyed him; and then, at the command of King Alcinous, all the noblemen of the city came together at the palace for a banquet in honour of Odysseus. There was food and wine in plenty, and talking and much laughter, and when the feasting was over, Alcinous bade the minstrel sing. 'Come, Demodocus, and sing for us some tale of old heroic deeds, for without your sweet voice no festivity would be complete.'

And someone led forth Demodocus and placed a stool for him in their midst, and put in his hands his lyre; for Demodocus was blind, though he had the sweetest voice in all Phaeacia. When he had plucked a few chords, Demodocus began to sing, and in the hall everyone else fell silent. He sang of the quarrel Odysseus and Achilles had once had when the Greeks were besieging Troy, and of the joy of the great king, Agamemnon, who led the Grecian host, when he saw the heroes wrangling. For it had been foretold to him that it would be a good omen for the Greeks if two of their best warriors should fall to quarrelling with each other.

The Phaeacians heard the minstrel's song with pleasure; but to Odysseus it brought only sorrow. For he remembered the old quarrel and the days at Troy, his comrades who had died there, and brave young Achilles with his long yellow hair and his quick temper, whose spirit he had seen in Hades' land when he went there to ask counsel of Teiresias; and he held his cloak before his face, that his tears might not be seen.

But Alcinous observed his grief and wondered at it, and instantly he rose. 'My friends and counsellors,' he said, 'we have feasted long and pleased our hearts with music, now let us return to the place of assembly and there display to the stranger our skill in wrestling, boxing, and running, that when he is once more in his own home he may speak of us to his friends and tell them how we excel in all manner of games.'

While King Alcinous, with Odysseus and the other older

noblemen, sat upon the stone seats in the assembly place, the young men of Phaeacia gathered on the stretch of sandy ground before them, eager to display their skill. And among them were three of the king's five sons, Halius, Clytoneus, and his favourite, Laodamas.

First came the foot-race, and at the word of command, the young men sped back and forth across the course until the full distance of the race was reached in a cloud of sand, and Clytoneus was proclaimed the winner.

The wrestling contests came next, and when lots had been drawn to pair off the opponents, the lithe antagonists twisted and struggled, and tripped and threw each other on the ground; and if a wrestler fell three times, his rival gained the victory. It was soon plain to see that a certain handsome young nobleman, Euryalus, excelled all the others, throwing first his own adversary, and then, one after the other, the victors from the other pairs.

After the wrestling was done, a space was marked out for the leaping, a long jump over a level stretch of ground. Here each youth held a metal weight, and after running a few paces to the mark, jumped, swinging his arms well forward with the weights, and where he touched the ground a peg was set.

Next the young men tried their skill at throwing the discus. They stood in spaces marked out by lines in the sand, holding the heavy metal plates high above their heads and swinging their arms down and forwards to throw the discus with all their strength as far as it would go.

The last contest of all was boxing. With thongs of ox-hide bound about their hands, the young men fought in pairs until one fell, and to Alcinous' great delight,

Laodamas was easily the victor here, swiftly striking down all his opponents.

While he was receiving the congratulations of his friends on his success, it came to the mind of Laodamas to say to them, 'Why do we not ask the stranger if he would care to join in any of our games? He is not so young as we, but he looks a fine strong man, he might be glad to try his strength.'

'That is well thought of, Laodamas,' said Euryalus, the handsome youth who had been winner in the wrestling, 'go now and challenge him.'

So Laodamas went to Odysseus and spoke to him with courtesy. 'Stranger, I know not if there is any among the contests at which you may excel, nor indeed whether you have a mind to games at all, but any one of us would welcome a trial with you, should you care for it. I know that you are eager to reach your home, but such a brief delay could make but little difference.'

Good-humouredly and with a smile, Odysseus answered him, 'I fear you must wish to laugh at me, Laodamas, that you offer me this challenge. I have been through too many misfortunes in the past years to have a mind to contests now. My only thought and care at this time is for my home and that I may return to it.'

Laodamas was about to speak again in polite acceptance of Odysseus' words, but Euryalus, who had followed him and was standing near, had caught Odysseus' answer and now spoke with scorn. 'Indeed, stranger, it was but a foolish thing to challenge you, for you do not look to me like a man well skilled in contests and men's games. You seem rather to be a merchant, one who travels from port to port with his merchandise, hurrying his sailors across the sea, lest a good bargain may be lost.'

Odysseus instantly grew angry. 'Young man,' he said, 'one should not judge by appearances alone. To but few men are all the gifts given. One may be a poor, inferior creature, yet when he speaks there is in his words all the wisdom in the world, and his speaking may move whole assemblies and persuade them to his way of thinking. While another may be as beautiful as the immortal gods, yet his speech may show naught but folly and an empty head. So, I think, it is with you. You are very handsome, no one could deny it, yet you have but little wits. I would tell you that when I was younger I was accounted among the best in contests of all kinds, but after all that I have suffered I have no heart for games. Yet in spite of that will I prove my words, for your discourtesy has made me angry.'

And with that Odysseus jumped up, not even throwing aside his cloak, and going to where a discus lay that no one had cast, for it was larger and heavier than the rest, he snatched it up; and hampered as he was by his mantle, he flung it from him along the course, and it fell far beyond the pegs that marked the other throws.

There was a great murmur of admiration among the watchers, and Odysseus, no longer so angry, smiled. 'Come now, you young men,' he called, 'and beat that if you can. Or if you would prefer, make test of me with wrestling or with boxing, even with running if you will, and I can promise you that I will acquit myself with credit. For I am well skilled in all manner of contests; yes, and in all fighting too, for I can shoot an arrow and cast a spear farther than most men. Indeed, it is only in the foot-race that I fear I might not be the winner, for I am no longer quite so young as once I was, and speed goes hand in hand with youth. Come, all you young Phaeacians, I am waiting for you.'

But there was no one there who answered his challenge, for they believed his boasts, having had a little proof of them in his throwing of the discus.

And at length Alcinous spoke, 'It does not surprise me, stranger, that you should have been angered at the ungracious words that Euryalus spoke to you. But come, forget them, and sit by me and I will show you something to remember when you are home again, something you may praise to your family and friends. For though we Phaeacians may not be the greatest boxers or wrestlers in the world, there are two things in which we excel all others, in seamanship and dancing. Of our skill in the former you will soon have proof, when in a Phaeacian ship you sail to your home, so come now and watch our dancing, and I promise you it will be a sight that you will remember with admiration all your days.'

Willingly, Odysseus took his place beside the king, while the young men and boys gathered on the level ground before them and took their places for the dance. Blind Demodocus was led to a chair in the centre of the dancing-floor, and there he sat, feeling carefully the seven strings of his lyre and tuning them to see that they were tightly strung. When the dancers were ready, someone touched him on the shoulder and spoke to him, and with a happy smile he began to play.

The tune was light and joyous, well suited to the dancers' mood and to their swiftly moving feet, and while he played, Demodocus sang a gay tale about the immortal gods; how Ares, fierce god of war and battles, loved gentle Aphrodite, goddess of love and beauty.

Odysseus watched, marvelling at the grace and skill of the young dancers, for never had he seen dancing so accomplished and so faultless. It was indeed a sight he would remember all his days, and when the dance was over he made haste to tell Alcinous so.

King Alcinous was delighted by his guest's enjoyment. 'But you have not yet seen all,' he said. And he called out Laodamas and Halius, his sons, and bade them dance the ball-dance for Odysseus. 'For of all our dancers there are none like them,' he said to him proudly.

The two young men took their places, surrounded by the other youths who clapped in rhythm to their dance. From one to another Halius and Laodamas passed a purple ball, twisting their bodies this way and that; bending backwards for a throw or leaping upwards for a catch and never missing. Their feet seemed to flash and twinkle in the very air, and they themselves to be no more things of the earth than the ball which they never once dropped to the ground in all the length of their dance; passing it from one to the other, while the clapping hands marked the rhythm of their measured movements, ever more loudly and ever more fast. Until at last, in one wild burst of sound and motion, the dance came to an end.

Odysseus turned to Alcinous. 'Indeed,' he said, 'never in my life have I seen a sight so graceful and so pleasing. Truly, not only in all Phaeacia, but in all the world, have your two sons no equal in the dance.'

Gladdened by Odysseus' heartfelt praise, King Alcinous

rose and spoke to the Phaeacians. 'My friends and counsellors,' he said, 'the stranger has been pleased to praise our dancing and speak gracious words of it. The time will soon be here when he must leave us, to return to his own land. When he departs from our shores, let it be with gifts from all of us, that in his home he may ever have works made by our craftsmen to remind him of Phaeacia.'

To this they all agreed, and straightway every noble there sent to his home that he might make a present to Odysseus. And Euryalus, repenting of his discourtesy, was the first to bring his gift, a bronze sword of fine workmanship, with a hilt of silver, and a scabbard of carved ivory.

'Stranger,' he said, 'I beg of you to take this sword in proof that you have forgiven my unmannerly and disrespectful words. May you forget them, and when you look upon it, remember only the well-wishes of the giver.'

Odysseus smiled and took the sword. 'All that has passed between us before this moment, Euryalus, is forgotten, and I remember of the giver of this goodly sword, only that he was a young nobleman of Phaeacia, handsome above all others, and well skilled at games.' And he slung the sword about his shoulder by its strap of patterned leather.

And one by one the nobles of Phaeacia brought him gifts; cups of polished gold and silver, mixing bowls of bronze, jars of wine, fine woven tunics and embroidered cloths, belts of silver links, golden brooches and brazen pins to fasten garments, three-legged cauldrons, and many other gifts beside. All these things King Alcinous' servants carried to the palace where they were packed in carved and painted wooden chests; and to their number Alcinous and Arete added many gifts of their own.

Alcinous called the Phaeacians to one final feast in honour of his guest, and they gathered together in the great hall, a festive crowd.

As he passed to the hall for the banquet, Odysseus saw Nausicaa watching him from the shadows beside one of the pillars of the door. He stood by her for a moment and she looked away from him, and then looked back again, and with a little smile she spoke. 'Think of me sometimes when you are in your home, for of all the Phaeacians it was I who helped you first.'

With gentleness and with sincerity Odysseus answered her, 'If it is granted me to see once more my home, then shall I ever remember you when I am there, and to me shall you be as one of the immortal goddesses, and I shall offer you my prayers all the days of my life. For it was you who returned that life to me.' And he went from her into the bright torch-light and gay laughter of the hall.

All welcomed him with kindness, and once again his chair was placed next to that of King Alcinous himself, and for him were reserved the best portions of all the dishes, such as are offered to the most honoured guests.

And a thought came to Odysseus, how he would like to hear the blind minstrel sing once more of Troy and the valorous deeds of the Greeks, although the memory of them brought so much pain to him. So, cutting a thick slice from the portion of roast pork that had just been set before him, he handed it on a silver platter to a serving-man, bidding him take it with his greetings to Demodocus. 'Tell him,' said Odysseus, 'that above all men I honour the makers of songs, for it is they who celebrate in poetry and music the deeds of men that might otherwise be forgotten utterly.'

And when the feasting was over, Odysseus sent again to the minstrel and begged him, for his sake, to sing once more of the Greeks who fought at Troy. 'This time,' he said, 'I would ask that you might relate, if you know the tale, how the wooden horse was taken into Troy, and how the city fell.'

Demodocus at once sounded his lyre, and when the hall was hushed, in his sweet voice he began the story. He told of how the wooden horse was fashioned, and of how the Greeks set fire to their own camp and sailed away in pretended raising of the siege. He told of how the Trojans came and dragged the horse into their city, and there debated what to do with it. 'For a full day,' he sang, 'from the rising to the setting of the sun, they argued whether it were best to break open the great wooden beast lest there should come danger to them from within; or whether to drag it forth from the city again and cast it from the cliffs into the sea below; or whether to accept the horse as a sign of victory to them, and let it stand in the assembly place, as an offering to the gods. And at sunset, it was this final counsel that prevailed, and the Trojans departed to their homes; and in the midst of the city, unguarded, stood the wooden horse. And then,' went on Demodocus, 'as soon as it was dark and the city lay in sleep, from the side of the hollow horse, stole forth the Grecian warriors and slipped silently through the streets. They fell upon the Trojans, bearing death with them, and though they were outnumbered, the victory was theirs. Many were the brave deeds of the Greeks that night and great was their courage, but the valour and the deeds of none surpassed those of Odysseus, king of Ithaca, the most subtle of all men. For Odysseus went with Menelaus, king of Sparta, for whose sake, that he might regain his wife, stolen by a Trojan prince, the war was fought, to the house of Deiphobus, son of the king of Troy, where lodged lovely Helen, Menelaus' wife. There they fought with Deiphobus, and Odysseus, well-nigh slain against enormous odds, in the end won victory and honour, for he was a mighty warrior and peerless among the Greeks.'

So sang Demodocus, and remembering, Odysseus wept; and Alcinous saw his tears and bade the minstrel sing no more. 'For', he said, 'your song has grieved our guest, and that must not be. Come, fill up the cups with wine and let us drink and be merry, for that is the fittest way to honour any guest.' Then turning to Odysseus, he said, 'Stranger, soon you will be gone from us, and our wishes for your safe homecoming and our gifts will go with you. Before you leave our city, if it is pleasing to you, will you not tell us your name and your homeland? For indeed, this last you will have to tell to our sailors who will row you there. It seems to me most likely from your sorrow at the minstrel's words, that you were one of those who fought at Troy. Why does the name of that fair and hapless city bring so much grief to you? Did you lose a kinsman there? Or perchance a brother? Or perhaps it was your own dear friend? For a kind and understanding friend can be nearer even than a brother.'

'Indeed, good King Alcinous,' Odysseus replied, 'it is, as you say, meetest at a banquet to drink the good wine and laugh. Grief has no place at a feast, and I have had grief enough in my day. Yet you ask me to relate my woes to you. So let it be. You are my host, it would be churlish to refuse, for a better host it would be hard to find. You ask my name. I am Odysseus, king of Ithaca, even that same Odysseus of whom your clear-voiced minstrel sang but now. Ithaca is only a small island, yet it is my home and very dear to me. It is a rugged land, with narrow ways and no broad roads, and its pasture-land is best fitted for the sturdy sure-footed goats. But yet it breeds fine men, brave and bold, and I long once more to see it, because, my friends, it is my home.'

Then, one by one, Odysseus related all his adventures. He told of the Lotus-eaters and the Cyclops, Polyphemus; and of the cruel Laestrygonian giants; and he told of Circe on her isle. He spoke of how he sailed into Hades' land; and of how he heard the Sirens sing and braved dread Scylla and Charybdis. And with grief he told of the slaying of the cattle of the sun, and the loss of his dear companions.

'And then, my friends,' he said, 'for seven years I was held in captivity on the island of Ogygia, where the nymph Calypso dwells. From thence I came on a raft across the tempestuous sea, and so landed on your kindly shores. And this, I pray, may be the end of all my wanderings.'

They heard him with amazement, and in silence sat watching him when he had finished, marvelling that they saw before their eyes a man who had lived through so many perils.

But Odysseus had talked far into the night, and Alcinous bade his noblemen and counsellors go home. 'Tomorrow,' he said, 'let all of you come here to speed the great Odysseus on his way. And though we have shown our friendship for him with gifts already, let each of us bring him a further present in the morning.'

To this they all willingly assented, and then went to their own homes, talking with wonder about Odysseus as they went.

Early in the morning their gifts were borne to the palace; great bowls with feet, silver cups and cauldrons, and many other treasures. When they had been carefully packed away in chests, they were carried to the harbour where the ship was waiting that was to carry Odysseus home; and King Alcinous himself watched them stowed away beneath the benches where the rowers sat.

Then after Odysseus had given his thanks to all, and waited once more on Queen Arete, he bade his kind host farewell, and went on board the ship. There the young men who were to row him home spread a rug and blankets for him on the deck, that he might sleep in comfort all through the tedious voyage. And while they rowed smoothly and swiftly through the blue water, with all the skill of a true seafaring folk, Odysseus slept.

He slept all that day and all through the night, and when on the following dawn, they sighted Ithaca, he still slumbered on. Being unwilling to waken him, they lifted him gently to the shore, still wrapped in the warm blankets, and left him on the sandy beach, his gifts all piled around him. Then quietly they put out to sea again.

But Poseidon, mighty god of all the oceans, had seen them take Odysseus safely to his own land at last, and he grew angry. And when the Phaeacian ship was within sight of home, he lifted up his hand through the water, and laying it upon the keel, turned her into a black rock, so that ever after people might wonder at it.

PART TWO

Telemachus seeks Tidings of his Father

VIII

Athene in Ithaca

AT about the time Odysseus was sailing from Ogygia on the raft that he had made, Athene, wisest of all the immortal goddesses, left the cloudy heights of Mount Olympus and went to the island of Ithaca. There, in the likeness of a traveller of middle years, she walked towards Odysseus' house.

The house was built of great blocks of grey stone, and, as was only fitting for the home of a king, was the finest in all Ithaca, with a wide courtyard surrounded by a high wall wherein stood two large wooden gates. Inside the courtyard, up against the wall, leant stalls for housing the beasts brought in from the farms, and kennels for the hounds; and near to them a flock of geese stepped solemnly, picking up corn and barley from the ground, or drinking, with uptilted heads, water from a trough. There, too, stacked against the wall were piles of wood and logs for fires; while towards the centre of the court, covered over with a roof of thatch to protect it from the dust, stood the well.

The house had a porch with four tall pillars, wide enough for several men to sit at ease beneath its pleasant shade and talk. Beyond the polished wooden doors of the house and leading into the great hall lay the vestibule, where guests and strangers slept. Down the great hall itself ran two rows of pillars to support the roof, and the wide hearth was in the very centre. Half-way along one side wall of the hall was a door opening into a covered passage-way which led to the store-room; while at the farthest end of the great room, opposite the entrance, was another door, this one leading to all the other rooms of the house and to the stairs which went up to the apartments of Penelope the queen.

Athene reached the house at the time when the evening meal was being prepared, and she stood on the threshold of the gates at the entrance to the courtyard waiting till she should be noticed.

Sitting in the porch there were a number of young men. They were playing draughts, throwing dice, or idly chatting to pass the time away until supper should be ready. Leaning against one of the pillars, with his arms folded, watching and listening to them with disapproval, stood a youth of some nineteen years of age, Telemachus, Odysseus' son. Slim and handsome and very like his father in appearance, this was the son whom Odysseus had left at home, a tiny babe, when he sailed for Troy.

Looking up for a moment, Telemachus saw, standing at the gates, a man whom he had never seen before; of middle age, with a face roughened by the winds and the sun, his cloak wrapped round him, he stood leaning on his spear.

'It is a shame that a stranger should stand outside the gates,' thought Telemachus. 'So long as there is any food left with which to welcome travellers, this house shall offer hospitality as though its master were at home.' And he ran across the courtyard to Athene, waiting at the gates.

'Greetings, stranger,' said Telemachus, 'you are welcome. Will you not come into the house and eat with me and rest?' And he led Athene across the courtyard, past the young men in the porch, and through the vestibule and on into the hall, taking her spear from her and standing it against a pillar, along with others belonging to his father.

The servants were making ready the supper, setting out chairs and tables, strewing fresh rushes on the floor, and mixing in heavy silver bowls the rich wine they poured from jars of painted earthenware.

Telemachus called to one of them to bring food and drink at once for him and for his guest, and placed two chairs and a table in a quiet corner of the great room. 'It will be full of noise in the hall when the others come in to eat,' he said, 'and perhaps an older man such as you are might prefer to avoid the company of boisterous young men.'

'You are thoughtful,' said Athene as she sat, 'and I thank you.'

Telemachus sat down beside her, and together they ate and drank; Athene noting with approval the courtesy of Odysseus' son; while Telemachus thought how later he might question the stranger to see if he could give him any news of his lost father.

Soon the evening meal was ready, and summoned by Medon, the herald of Odysseus, the young men came in from the porch and took their places in the hall, laughing and talking, and they were quickly joined by others who came up from the town. The whole company of them, more than a hundred in all, ate and drank and called to one another across the room, shouting out the latest news from the town and telling how they had spent the day, not even keeping silence when Phemius, the minstrel, sang.

Telemachus watched them angrily from where he sat with the stranger; until, no longer able to forbear from speaking of them, he complained, 'One might think it was their own food they were eating so greedily, and their own wine they were quaffing. How I long that the lord of this house might come home one day soon and drive them forth, every one.' He recovered himself and smiled. 'But I am being ungracious to a guest, you must forgive me, stranger. Will you not tell me your name and from whence you come?'

'My name is Mentes,' Athene answered, 'and I am a leader among the Taphians. My travels having brought me near to Ithaca, I thought that I might see whether my old friend Odysseus still lived and prospered. I know this is his house, and from your likeness to him, I think that you must be his son. Tell me, am I not right in this?'

'You are indeed,' replied Telemachus. 'You see in me the son of that most unlucky man. For of all the Greeks who sailed to fight at Troy, he is the only one who neither lived to reach his home, nor died, honoured by his comrades, on the battlefield. It is now close on ten years since Troy fell, and yet my father has not come home, and I and my mother have no word of him, whether he still lives or whether he has died in some far-off land.'

'Indeed, good youth, I do pity you, and I do pity the noble Odysseus. But remembering the man and his courage and his resourcefulness, I have no doubt that, if he lives, at the last he will come safely home. But what means this feasting in Odysseus' house? This jubilation in the absence of the master? Is this a wedding these young men are celebrating, or some other important occasion of rejoicing? Have you yourself called them together for a banquet?' asked Athene, knowing full well the answer.

'It is no wedding they are celebrating, though they wish it were,' said Telemachus with bitterness. 'And they are no guests of mine, being here uninvited, eating my father's meat and drinking his good wine and making free with his possessions as though the house were theirs. No, I have not called them together, and though I would, I cannot send them hence; for I am only young, and unused to commanding men older than myself, having until but lately been considered no more than a child. And they will not listen to courteous suggestions that they should go back to their own homes until my mother has made up her mind. For you must know they are my mother's suitors, all the unmarried young noblemen of Ithaca and the lords from the islands around. From Dulichium, from Same, and from the forests of Zacynthus have they come to gather here in my father's house. For though we have heard no word of his death, they have chosen to consider that he never will come home and that my mother is a widow, to be courted by another husband. For she is still young, and not without much beauty, and she is renowned throughout all Ithaca and the islands for her virtues and her prudence, and many a man would be proud to have her for his wife. But my mother, like myself, still hopes that one day Odysseus may return; and so she remains in his house, waiting and hoping, and will not give an answer to her wooers. And they say that since she will not decide among them, they will come here every day to make certain that they are not absent when she at last comes to a decision. Besides, they find it cheap and pleasant, to live on my father's food, ordering his servants as they will, and passing their days in idleness in the house of a king. And because I am young they will not hear me when I speak of it, but only laugh and tell me I should be glad to have a mother so beautiful and so accomplished that many men desire to marry her.'

'It is indeed a sorry tale you tell,' said Athene, 'and you have my sympathy, young man. I am ashamed to think that in these islands, and above all, in Ithaca itself, the home of my good Odysseus, there are so many men who could act so shamelessly. But take courage, my friend, for I am certain that your father will return, and when he does, it will be an unhappy day for these young men who feast so joyously tonight.'

'I thank you for your consoling words,' replied Telemachus, sighing, 'but waiting is not easy, and what if, after all, my father should never return?'

'I am an older man than you, and I have seen more of life,' Athene said, laying a kindly hand upon his arm. 'If you will not resent advice from a stranger, let me give some good advice to you. Show yourself a true son of Odysseus, as I remember him to be. Do not wait for his return, but try to drive away these rogues yourself.

Tomorrow, go to the place of assembly in the town and call together all the elders and counsellors, the noblemen and the lords, and put your case to them. Tell them openly and plainly how the suitors are wasting your father's goods and making free with his possessions. Then, when you see that there are those among the staider and wiser men of Ithaca who would support you, ask these suitors of your mother to begone to their own homes, there to wait her answer as well-behaved wooers should.'

Telemachus' eyes grew bright and he clenched his fists. 'Noble Mentes,' he said, 'I will do as you bid me. Perchance they will listen to me if I speak to them before the assembled men of Ithaca.'

'And after—hear me further—'went on Athene, 'fit out a small ship of some twenty oars and sail to Pylos, in the south, and there ask good Nestor, that wise old king, if he has news of your father. For Nestor fought at Troy with Odysseus, and so did Nestor's son, and it may well be that he has heard word of your father since he set forth from that city. And then go on from Pylos to Sparta, it is but two days' journey in a fast chariot, and there seek news from King Menelaus, and from Queen Helen, for whose sake the war was fought. They also may have words of comfort for you.'

'I will do even as you tell me, good stranger,' said Telemachus with eagerness. 'It well may be some gain will come of it.'

'And if it does not,' said Athene, 'if perhaps you should hear that your father is dead, then you will at least have learnt the worst there is to know. And if you should hear no news of him at all, why then, no harm will have come of it, and you will but have tried to solve your troubles, and you can wait perhaps another year in the patient hope that Odysseus may return. But if in twelve months he is not here, then you can consider him as dead, and urge your mother to take another husband and go to another home, leaving you in possession of your inheritance.'

Thus Athene spoke, for she wished to try Telemachus, whether he was a son worthy of his father, the wily Odysseus, schemer of many plots.

Telemachus, his young face flushed with enthusiasm, and his eyes shining, jumped to his feet so eagerly that one or two of the suitors marked his movements, though they could not hear his words, and wondered at him. 'Your counsel is good, and I will do even as you say,' he said. 'Stranger, I thank you with all my heart.'

Athene rose. 'It is well,' she said, 'and may your misfortunes soon be at an end and your noble father see once more his home. But now it grows late, the sun is setting, and I must be on my way. Farewell, brave son of Odysseus, good luck in all your ventures be with you.'

'Noble Mentes, will you not tarry here awhile? It is a father's advice and help such as you have this evening given me that I have lacked so long. I would be both pleased and honoured if you would remain as my guest for a few days.'

Athene smiled and shook her head. 'I thank you, Telemachus, but I would be gone tonight.'

'Stay at least until I have had time to find you a worthy gift to take with you,' pleaded Telemachus. 'No ordinary guest should leave a house without a present from his host. How much more should the giver of such serviceable counsel as yours receive a fitting gift at his departure?'

'No, Telemachus, seek not to keep me longer here, for I must be gone. Farewell, and remember all that I have said to you.' And in an instant Athene had vanished and Telemachus stood alone beside the chairs that they had used.

Marvelling, he thought, 'That was indeed one of the immortal gods, no mortal man could vanish thus. I have been honoured by a visitor from Mount Olympus, surely that betokens good fortune to the house?'

Phemius, the young minstrel, was once again singing, and lest it should be questioned that he sat alone, Telemachus moved closer to the suitors and took a chair among them to listen to the song.

Phemius sang of the return of the Greeks from Troy, and his voice rang so sweetly throughout the hall, that even the noisy suitors were silenced, and heard him with admiration. One of the servants had left open the door which led to the other rooms of the house and to the women's quarters, so the sound of the minstrel's singing reached up the stairs to Penelope the queen, where she sat spinning sadly among her serving-maids. She heard his words plainly, of how the Greeks, victorious and triumphant, set sail from the fallen city, their ships well packed with spoils; and her eyes filled with bright tears as she remembered Odysseus, who had sailed, but not yet come home.

She rose and laid aside her distaff, and beckoning two of the maidens to attend her, she came down the stairs and entered the hall. She stood awhile upon the threshold of the door with tears on her cheeks; until at last she could bear her thoughts no longer, and her clear voice called to Phemius across the hall, and bade him cease his singing.

'Phemius, you know many songs, on many different

themes. Sing one of them, if these young men must have music while they feast. But tell no more the tale of the Greeks' return from Troy, for one good man I know of, who left that unhappy city, did not come back to his home and his unfortunate wife; even my own dear husband, Odysseus.'

The song failed upon the minstrel's lips and his lyre fell silent, while the wooers gazed with surprise and admiration at Penelope where she stood by the door, and she drew a fold of her coloured veil across her face.

Telemachus saw in her arrival and her words a chance to impress the suitors with his new-born resolution to assert himself. 'Dear mother,' he said gently, 'let Phemius sing of what he will. Of all the noble warriors who fought at Troy, there were many who did not return, for they had found graves in Trojan earth. Odysseus was not alone ill fated. And it is not the fault of Phemius but the will of the immortal gods that these things came to pass, so do not blame him that he sings of them. It is now almost twenty years since my father sailed for Troy and left me, a tiny babe, in your arms. Today I am no longer a child. Good mother, I beg you, go back to your spinning, and leave me to order my father's house.'

Penelope was amazed to hear him speak thus, and pleased at his words, both because she was proud that her son should have shown himself to be no more a child and should have spoken with authority, and because she hoped that if he displayed a determined spirit, the suitors might be inclined to respect a little more her absent husband's property. So without another word, she turned away and left the hall, followed by her serving-maids, smiling a little

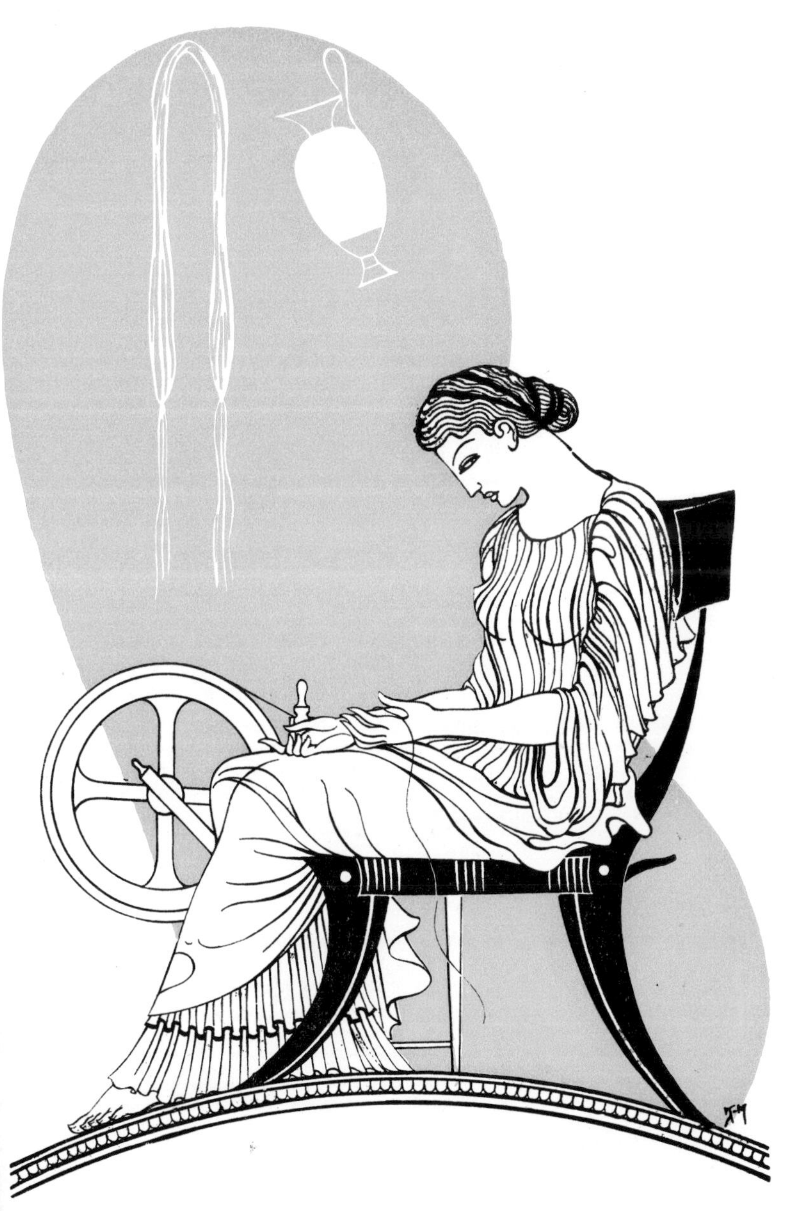

to herself as she went, and thinking, 'May Telemachus prove himself as good a man as his dear father, for this house has been too long without a master.'

But it was with annoyance that the suitors heard Telemachus speak, and they glanced at each other, with eyebrows raised and shoulders shrugging, and here and there a whispered word of mockery. But they said nothing out aloud, for each feared that Penelope might hear him and be angered, and his suit would thus not prosper.

When his mother had left the room, Telemachus turned to his uninvited guests. 'For tonight,' he said, 'let us feast and listen to the singing, since tomorrow I mean to call together the townspeople at the assembly place, as is my right as the son of your king. There will I ask you before all the gathered citizens to return once more to your own homes, or to find your meals in some other house. For I am weary of the waste and gluttony that for ever goes on in this hall. If you are men of decent feeling, you will respect my wishes and depart, but if, even after I have demanded it before the people, you refuse to listen to my words, then may some evil fate befall you, and may you perish, every one, even though it be within my house.'

There was not one among the suitors who was not astonished to hear him speak so to them. For before that day he had been mild in speech and meek in manners when in their company; and they had grown used to considering him as a child whose wishes might be ignored and whose words left unheeded.

For a moment no one answered him, for they all knew that what he demanded was only just and right, though they had no intention of submitting. And then Antinous, the son of Eupeithes, a nobleman of Ithaca, who was the most insistent and the most arrogant of all the wooers, spoke with ugly scorn. 'Why, Telemachus, if you are, as you say, no longer a child, then I fear you have grown up into a shameless boaster and one who delights to pick a quarrel. And I can only hope, for the sake of all my peaceful fellow citizens, that you may never rule in Ithaca as our king.'

'Indeed, Antinous,' Telemachus retorted, 'I could think of many a worse fate than to be king here in Ithaca. Kings and their houses and their goods are held in honour and treated with respect, and I could be glad of a little more deference and consideration.' He paused a moment and then added bitterly, 'Though of late it has seemed to me that however deserving he may be of them, even the best of kings loses that honour and respect which are his due, unless he is present to enforce the paying of them.' He went on, emboldened by the visit of a goddess, his voice raised in defiance of them for the first time since they had come to his father's house, 'But who shall be king in Ithaca, once it is proved Odysseus lives no more, is not for me or for you to decide. Yet whoever is king of the island, I intend to be master in this house.'

Antinous glowered at him in anger, but Eurymachus, a suitor no whit less disagreeable than Antinous, but with a smoother tongue, said pleasantly, calming the uneasy moment, 'You are not mistaken, Telemachus. It is not for any of us here to decide who shall succeed your honoured father. But as for you, who would deny to you the right to be lord in your own house? The rights of each man, that is something we would willingly see upheld, and now that you are of an age to manage your own matters, we would gladly see you paid your due respect.' Then, because Eurymachus suspected that Telemachus' sudden change of manner towards his mother's suitors might in some way be owing to the visit of a stranger to the house that day, he asked, easily, and as though the answer mattered very little to him, 'But to talk of happier things than the sad loss of your father, tell us, Telemachus, who was the stranger who supped with you? He seemed a man of some distinction, and he disappeared so suddenly—one moment here, and the next time I looked, vanished utterly—that I had no chance to have speech with him. Did he perchance have any news of Odysseus?'

For a moment Telemachus was silent, then because he was his father's son, he answered subtly, 'Indeed, Eurymachus, I begin to fear my father never will come home. Unlike my dear mother, I am fast losing all hope of seeing him again. The stranger was no more than an old friend of his, one Mentes, from Taphos.'

'From Taphos?' said Eurymachus, 'Would that I had spoken to him.'

But Antinous threw aside the golden cup which he had just drained, so that it rolled, ringing, on the floor. 'We have had enough talking of old fools from Taphos. Come, let us dance.' He rose. 'Strike up your lyre, Phemius, and give us a gay tune.'

The minstrel played for them, and thrusting aside the chairs and tables, the suitors danced. Telemachus watched them for a little space with hatred in his heart, and then he turned and left the hall through the door at the far end, calling as he went to Eurycleia, his old nurse, who had been nurse also to Odysseus, when he too had been a child. 'Bring me a light, Eurycleia, I am sickened with the sight of those shameless rogues. I can be with them no longer. Light me a lamp in my own room.'

He lay awake upon his bed for hours, thinking over all that Athene had said to him, and resolving in his mind the words that he should speak before the assembly on the morrow.

But the suitors danced and drank until far into the night, then one by one they drifted from the house; the Ithacans to their own homes, and the other island princes to their lodgings in the town.

IX

The Assembly

As soon as it was morning, Telemachus sent forth heralds from Odysseus' house to call together all the noblemen and leaders of Ithaca for an assembly. It was the first conclave of the townspeople of that island that had been called since Odysseus, their king, had sailed for Troy, and they were much surprised at the summons. Wondering, they gathered in the place of assembly in the centre of the town, old men and young men; and because Odysseus had been gone for twenty years, a few among them were young enough for this to be their first public assemblage.

Some came eagerly and asking questions of all their friends as to why they had been called together. 'It is the first time for twenty years,' they said. 'What of importance can have occurred?'

Some paced slowly and with dignity and replied to all questioners with a solemn shake of their heads, as though they knew full well why the summons had gone forth, but considered the matter too grave for light discussion before the meeting. 'After the assembly, my friend, after the assembly will I tell you. These things should first be debated publicly,' they would answer.

Yet others came reluctantly and with annoyance, grumbling as they came, 'We have had no assembly for almost twenty years, why should we have been called together on today of all days. I was going to walk early from the town to my farm in the hills to see how things went there. I am certain that my steward has been cheating me,' or, 'My wife's brother lies sick upon the island of Zacynthus, I should have sailed this morning to see how he fares.'

And so they came together, taking their places on the stone seats in the early morning sunshine; and among them were all those of Penelope's wooers whose home was Ithaca, and they alone of all the citizens knew why the assembly had been called and by whom. But they were silent, answering no questions and offering to speak to no one save among themselves.

When the appointed time had come, and the townspeople were all gathered, Telemachus left his home and walked to the assembly place. In a gleaming white tunic and wearing a purple cloak with a yellow striped border and a yellow fringe, his long curls bound up by a garland of ribbon, his sword slung about his shoulders and a spear in his hands, with his two favourite hounds at his heels, he looked a youth whom Odysseus might well have been proud to call his son, had he been there to see him. He was excited and a little afraid, but none of this he showed, as with apparent calm he took his place, greeting gravely and with courtesy all who were present.

And the older men there, who had known Odysseus as a youth, whispered to each other, 'He has grown up into a fine young man, so very like his father was, at the same age,' and, 'I wish our king were here today to see his handsome son.'

For a while they sat expectantly, now that their numbers were complete; then an old nobleman, very bent and frail, rose to his feet, and too feeble to leave his place for the speaker's stand in the centre of the assembly, spoke from where he stood, in a thin, cracked voice. 'My friends and fellow countrymen of Ithaca,' he said, 'this is the first assembly that has been called since our good king Odysseus sailed away to fight at Troy. Who among us here has called it, and why? Has he some news of importance to impart to us? Is it that he perhaps has heard that the king is coming home at last, or—may the gods forbid it—that he is dead? Whoever he is that has called us here, and whatever his news may be, let him show himself and declare his purpose.'

Telemachus instantly rose up, and leaving his spear propped against the seat, a hound crouched on either side of it, he stood out in the centre of the assembly place, and turning first to the old man who had spoken, he said, 'Noble lord, it was I, Telemachus, son of Odysseus, your king, who called this meeting of the men of Ithaca today. I have, alas, no news of Odysseus' return, nor, indeed, any public matters to report to you, my fellow citizens. My reason for calling this assembly here today is to speak to you on something that touches me alone.' He turned and looked around the gathering. 'My friends, and lords of Ithaca, hear my grievance and give me your support. Two great troubles have come upon me. The first is fate, and fate we cannot strive against. My father Odysseus, as you all do know, has not yet returned from Troy, though that city fell nigh on ten years ago and the war was ended. But in all that time have I had no word of him, whether he be alive or dead, and I have no means of telling if he will ever see his home again. This should surely be grief enough for any man, and as I have said, it is fate and there is no remedy in our hands for that. But my other grievance can and should be removed. My friends, ever since it seemed as though there were a chance that Odysseus might never again come home, my mother, the good Queen Penelope, has been harassed by scores of suitors. There is, it seems, not one young man in Ithaca or in our neighbouring isles who does not wish to marry her. But they are not content to wait upon her and bring her gifts at seemly intervals, handing them with fair words to her housekeeper, and lingering within her walls only long enough to drink a cup of wine and make a courteous greeting. No, these young men come in tens and scores, uninvited and without presents, and every day in my father's house they sit and eat and drink his food and wine, order his servants as though they were their own, call to his minstrel to sing to them, and in all things comport themselves as though they were at home. My mother is embarrassed by their presence, and I, her son, am slighted by them and treated as of no account in my own father's house; while Laertes, my grandfather, driven away by grief for the loss of his son, and by the insolence of these suitors, lives in misery on his farm across the hills. These daily ravages upon our stores and food are lessening my father's wealth; cattle are slaughtered to feed these men, wine-jars broken open to satisfy their never-ending thirst, his servants corrupted to neglect their duties, waiting day after day upon these wooers. This is no fitting way to behave towards the wife, or perchance the widow, of a king, and towards his only son, and I ask my mother's suitors, here, before all the assembled men of Ithaca, that they will cease to frequent my father's house, and conduct themselves as any self-respecting wooers should.' He stopped, and carried away by his unhappiness, he could not restrain his tears, so that there were many there who pitied him.

But Antinous jumped to his feet from where he sat beside his father, the Lord Eupeithes, his face dark with fury, his brows drawn together in a frown, and he shouted to Telemachus, 'You are a liar who would blacken the good name of your mother's suitors for your own ends. For I tell you, Telemachus, it is not our fault that we are kept idly loitering in your house. It is, and has always been, the fault of your scheming mother.'

Eurymachus, who sat on the other side of him, laid a restraining hand upon his wrist, but Antinous shook it off angrily without a glance, and went on, 'It is she who has kept us waiting for an answer, it is she who is delaying her choice of a husband, and that not openly or honestly. For years she has cheated us, cunningly and with fair words. Three years ago, when first we gathered at your house and pressed her for an answer to our wooing, she excused herself from making any choice with the plea that she was occupied with her spinning and her weaving. She said that she was making a shroud for old Laertes, King Odysseus' father; that when the time came for him to die, as all mortals must, he might have a winding-sheet fit for one of his high rank.

'"He is an old man," she said to us, "and I must not delay the work. When it is over, then will I name my choice of a husband from among you all."

'Would any man of honour not have respected her request? We suitors all agreed to wait until the work was finished, and for three years we waited while she spun and wove. All the mornings she spun the fine white wool, and all the afternoons she spent in weaving the yarn that she had spun; and then at night, when we had left the house and all the servants slept, she would rise up from her bed and unravel all that she had woven in the day. And so the months passed, month after month, and she worked industriously. Month after month she worked, but the skeins of wool piled up in her apartments and there was no shroud for Lord Laertes. One of her waiting-women told us of the queen's deception, how she played us false; and one night two or three of us returned to the house by darkness and surprised her at her task of unravelling her work. Her trick has been found out at last, and she must now complete the winding-sheet for her husband's father, but her craft has delayed us for three years. And yet, Telemachus, you dare to say that we suitors are at fault.' He paused for breath, and then went on more calmly, 'I say to you, Telemachus, and to all you other men of Ithaca, that never will we suitors leave Odysseus' house until Queen Penelope has made her choice among us. So long as she keeps us waiting, we shall remain in her home.' He looked round the assembly, 'Am I not right in that, and are we not all agreed, you fellow wooers of the queen?'

And at once, all those other suitors who were present, called out that they were in accord with what he said.

Antinous smiled with satisfaction at their agreement. 'So you see, young Telemachus, your only hope of being quit of us, is to persuade your mother to come to a decision, and marry once again.'

'She is my mother,' said Telemachus, 'and was the wife of a king. It is not fitting that I should try to persuade her in this matter, or hasten her to make a choice against her will. She loved my father dearly, and would not think it seemly to hurry to another's house, without even being sure that he is dead.'

Antinous made an impatient gesture and sat down and whispered to Eurymachus, and they both glanced up contemptuously at Telemachus.

Telemachus grew angry, and, as a young man will, he spoke without considering his words. 'I demand that all you insolent men shall leave my father's house this very day. For I swear that otherwise I shall pray to all the immortal gods that they send down a ghastly vengeance on you and destroy you utterly, every one of you.'

There was silence in the assembly at his bold words, though a few of the suitors murmured among themselves. Then one or two of them laughed aloud, mockingly, and whispered to each other, 'The little puppy is showing his teeth at last.' But there were several among the older men, who hearing him, nodded their approval.

At that moment two eagles soared up from the wooded heights of Mount Neriton, lying inland on the island, and wing outstretched to wing, they flew towards the town; two mighty birds, in perfect accord. But directly above the place of assembly they fell to fighting in the air, tearing at each other with hooked talons and curving beaks, scattering feathers to the wind and screeching angrily the while.

The men of Ithaca watched them in amazement, wondering what such an omen might foreshadow, for it was not every day that a similar sight was seen. Finally, the two eagles, still battling above the island, flew away eastwards, and their cries faded on the air.

'It is a portent,' whispered the people to one another. 'What can it signify?' And they debated among themselves as to the meaning.

Then Halitherses, an old nobleman who had once been known for his skill in prophecy and the interpretation of omens, both good and ill, rose up and spoke. 'Hear me now, you men of Ithaca, for I think that I can tell to you the meaning of the sight which we have all just seen. The thought is upon me that soon Odysseus, our king, will be home. When he sailed to Troy I foresaw that he would not return until twenty years had passed, and it is nigh on twenty years since he left our midst. Soon will he be back, and when he comes, then will it be an unhappy day for those that waste his substance in his house. That, my friends, is how I explain the fighting of these eagles above our town. Heed my warning, all you suitors of the queen, lest in the days to come you shall regret it.'

A few of the suitors seemed perturbed, and Antinous glowered angrily and seemed about to reply; but it was Eurymachus who answered with a laugh. 'Go home, good Lord Halitherses, and tell fortunes to amuse your grandchildren, but do not expect grown men to believe your prophecies. Why, I warrant myself as good a seer as you over this matter, and I say it bodes no ill. Besides, there are many birds which one may see, flying in the sky, if one only looks for them, yet but rarely does their flying signify disaster, or indeed, anything at all. No, sad as it is for our friend Telemachus, it seems plain by now that King Odysseus is dead and never will return to Ithaca. It is but heartless and shameful to seek to raise up false hopes in the lad's mind of his father's return, no doubt in the expectation of a reward from him and the queen. And ill indeed would it be to urge him to violent conduct against his fellow countrymen.' Then, turning to Telemachus, he said pleasantly, 'Come, my friend, forget your quarrel with us, and go home and persuade your mother that she is a widow, and that it is only right that she should gladden the house of another husband. Then shall your home be free of all her wooers, for, as Antinous has warned you, we shall all remain within your walls until she has chosen one of us. For she is a most excellent lady, and there is none among us who would give up hope of winning her while she yet hesitated to make up her mind.'

Telemachus then bethought himself of Athene's further advice to him, and silencing his anger, he answered quietly, 'Eurymachus and all you other suitors, I have stated my case before you and before all Ithaca, and you have made me your reply. You know my wishes, and I know your intentions. Let us not speak further of them here. I now propose to fit out a ship that I may sail from here to Pylos, where wise old King Nestor rules, and to the palace of King Menelaus in Sparta, and in those places ask tidings of my father. For Nestor had a son who died at Troy, and Menelaus was at the sacking of the city, perchance they both might tell me news of their one-time comrade. If the news is good, and there is still hope of Odysseus' return, then shall I continue to wait for him in patience. But if it seems certain that he is truly dead, then shall I return to Ithaca and build him a memorial, fit for the great and goodly king he was, and urge my mother to take another husband and go at last to another home.'

With this, Telemachus went back to his place and sat down once more. His two hounds stood and wagged their tails to see him come, and then lay at his feet.

Upon that Mentor rose, who had been a firm friend of Odysseus. 'People of Ithaca,' he said, 'I am grieved to see how easily a good man is forgotten. Odysseus was a just and kindly king, one who always had our benefit at heart, yet today not one of us has spoken up for his young son, who has but so lately reached man's estate. I expect but little merit from his mother's wooers, for they are blinded by the virtues and the beauty of our fair queen. But it is you others, you older men, whose silence offends me, for, save for Lord Halitherses' timely warning, you have uttered no single word of condemnation, nor attempted to restrain these young men, though your numbers are greater by far than theirs.'

One of the wooers instantly jumped to his feet. 'For shame, Mentor,' he cried, 'why do you seek to stir up strife? Shall grown men quarrel over a few plates of meat and jars of wine? Besides, it is Odysseus' food we eat, not yours, and therefore not your concern at all. And should Odysseus come home as you seem to wish, well,' he smiled unpleasantly, 'we suitors far outnumber him, and maybe after all, his wife would not have so much joy of his homecoming as she hopes. As for Telemachus, no one will prevent him from going to Pylos and to Sparta if he wishes. Indeed, it will be a pleasure not to have him sulking in the house, resenting our good appetites, for a few days at least. And doubtless you, Mentor, with old Halitherses ambling at your side, will be glad to go and bid him farewell at the harbour and wish him a successful voyage.' He paused and looked around him with insolence, then added, 'Truly, men of Ithaca, I should imagine that by now we have all said what we had to say, so let us consider the assembly ended, and go back to our homes.'

At once all the suitors rose, and in a group left the assembly place and went to the house of Odysseus for the midday meal. And after them, the other townsfolk also rose, and with much talk about the events of the morning, made their way back to their own homes.

But Telemachus went alone to the sea-shore, and there, standing upon the golden sands, he prayed to immortal Athene, that she might help him to get ready a ship to sail to Pylos and might prosper his voyage; and that in the end she might send his father safely home.

And all of these prayers Athene heard, and answered in due course.

X

King Nestor

WHEN Telemachus returned home it was nearing evening, and he found the suitors awaiting supper after having spent the afternoon at javelin-throwing in the courtyard. He tried to slip through them unobserved and go to his own quarters; but Antinous saw him and hurried forward with a smile and took his hand in a warm greeting.

'Why, here is Telemachus, our fiery orator. He is home at last,' he laughed, and laid a hand upon Telemachus' shoulder. 'Come, Telemachus, let us forget our wrangling of this morning, and let us feast in friendship as before. See, meat and drink are even now being set before us, come and sup with us here, and tell us all how you have passed the day since we parted in the place of assembly. But do not think to leave us yet to go to Pylos to seek tidings of your father. Some day, I have no doubt, will the men of Ithaca provide a ship for you to sail in where you please, but till then, let us enjoy the pleasant things in life, all of us, here together.'

But Telemachus snatched his hand away and said, 'Antinous, it is no longer possible for me to bear your company with any show of pleasure. When I was a child I suffered your insolence in silence, as befits a child. But I am a boy no longer, and I will not stand by unmoved while you waste my property before my eyes. And I am going to Pylos and to Sparta, to see King Nestor and King Menelaus, as soon as it can be brought to pass, and no word from you or any other man shall prevent me. And if at Pylos and at Sparta I can find no news that will drive you from the house, scattering for shelter from the anger of your king like leaves before the wind; then, when I return, in Ithaca itself shall I seek for a means of ridding my house of all you hated suitors, and I shall not rest till I have found it.' And he turned from Antinous and went across the hall.

But the suitors who had heard his words laughed and mocked him. 'Indeed, Telemachus is going to murder us, every man, the brave youth that he is,' said one.

Said another, 'He is going to Pylos to ask old Nestor's help, or perhaps he goes to Menelaus to ask for a Spartan army with which to kill his fellow countrymen in Ithaca.'

'No,' said yet another, laughing, 'I think it far more likely that our dear Telemachus will travel even farther afield and buy a deadly poison, and drop it in our wine when he comes home, he loves us so.'

While with pretended seriousness, another young man

called out, 'Perhaps he has inherited his father's knack of losing himself at sea, and so may be lost between here and Pylos. That would indeed be a sorry day for us, for we should have the tedious task of sharing out his possessions among ourselves. His cattle to some, to some his slaves, and to others his land, while this fine house would go to him who weds the fair Penelope. What irksome labour it would be for us.'

At this they all burst out laughing, and Telemachus, ashamed and angry, went through the door at the side of the great hall and made his way along the passage to the store-room of Odysseus, calling as he went for Eurycleia who kept the key. The old nurse came hurrying from the women's quarters, and unlocked the strong door for him, and together they went inside.

Here, in this wide room, were ranged the treasures of Odysseus; gold and silver cups and platters, wrought silver dishes, chased golden bowls for mixing wine, and polished brazen ewers and cauldrons. In wooden chests lay dyed and woven cloths and embroidered garments smelling of sweet spices; filmy scarves and dainty veils, fit for the queens of Ithaca, and plaited girdles for a slender waist. In little caskets of carved ivory or curious woods lay brooches, rings, and bracelets, and pins of bone and metal for pinning up a woman's hair.

Here, too, were kept the close-sealed wine-jars, on shelves along the walls, placed carefully in order of their vintage. Around the plump black crocks ran wreaths of leaves or twining flowers in yellow, red, or white; or here and there would be a jar which had a band of fishes swimming on a wavy sea, or a handsome pattern of lines and dots painted boldly in rich red. While on one shelf were collected flasks, both large and small, of scented oil for perfuming and anointing.

To one side of this treasure-chamber lay the armoury. Heavy spears and light javelins in stands against the wall, and shields piled upon the floor, swords laid carefully in their scabbards, and polished armour, shining brightly. And on the wall, upon a peg, hung the great bow of Odysseus, which he had left behind him when he sailed to Troy.

But Telemachus had not come to look at all his father's wealth, his mind was too full of troubled thoughts to give any heed to the treasures gathered here. He turned to the old woman. 'Nurse, fill me twelve jars with wine, the best we have, save for that special vintage which I know you are keeping to celebrate the day my father shall come home —may it be soon. Twelve jars of wine, well covered, and barley flour in leather bags, and have them ready by tonight for me. But say no word of this to any one, not even to my mother, for I am going to sail south to Pylos, and from there shall I journey on to Sparta, to see if I can learn tidings of my father, and I would not that any man should hinder me from my intentions.'

But Eurycleia cried out and flung her arms about his neck. 'My child, whatever made you think of doing such a thing? To go alone, all the way to Sparta. To travel half across the world and perchance never to come home again. Or if you do, to find these wicked men who ravage our home have planned some dreadful deed against you so that they may take what is rightly yours and enjoy it quite unchecked, without you to say them nay. No, no, my little one, stay here with us. No matter how hard life may be for you, it is always better for a young man to stay in his own home than to voyage over the seas.'

'Hush, nurse, Sparta is not so very far away, and I shall come back again, and soon; for I think that one of the immortal gods is with me in this. And, nurse, if I should be successful in finding good news, think how those men would run for their homes when they heard that Odysseus was coming back.' So he spoke to comfort her; but in his heart he doubted, after all that had passed that day, whether the suitors would be so easily driven from the house, even by Odysseus, should he ever return.

Eurycleia dried her eyes and sniffed. 'It seems but only the other day you were a little boy, playing at my knee, and now here you are, saying that you are going to Sparta, where great King Menelaus rules. But it is no use an old woman's speaking, for you will no longer listen to my advice, though you were glad enough to take it once.'

Telemachus put his arm around her. 'Nurse, dear old nurse, I may not be taking your advice today, but I am trusting you instead. Of all the servants in the house, I have chosen you to help me. Not even my mother am I telling of my plans, and you must promise me that you will keep the truth from her until, say, twelve days shall be passed, for I do not want her to grieve and fret herself for me. Let her think that I have gone to my grandfather on his farm, or to Philoetius the cowman, to see how our cattle increase on the mainland.'

'She would think it strange that you went either to Philoetius or to Lord Laertes without bidding her good-bye,' said Eurycleia doubtfully.

'That is how you must help me, nurse, by telling her a likely story to set her mind at ease. Come, dear old Eurycleia, promise me that you will aid me in the first important endeavour of my life, and say nothing about it to anyone.'

So Eurycleia promised him to keep silence; and she set to work to draw off the jars of wine, and fill the bags with barley meal, so that they should be ready for him when he needed them.

But Telemachus returned to the great hall and joined the suitors at their supper, and to calm any suspicions that they might have had, he talked and laughed with them, so that they thought he had forgotten his earlier angry words. But when dusk fell, he slipped from the hall, and aided by Athene, went through the town. There a kindly citizen named Noemon lent him willingly a small ship, and Athene gathered together for him a company of adventurous youths of his own age, who, encouraged by his friend Peiraeus, readily undertook to sail with him to Pylos.

Then, when the suitors had left Odysseus' house and gone to their own homes to sleep, Telemachus led his ship-mates back to the house. Quietly they entered the hall and gathered up the bags of flour and jars of wine from the place where good Eurycleia had left them, hidden behind a group of chairs, so that neither Penelope nor the other servants might see them, should any of them pass that way.

The youths returned quickly to the ship and stowed everything on board; then in the darkness they set sail for Pylos, and Athene herself gave them a fair breeze. All night long they sailed, and all the while Telemachus sat at the prow and watched through the dim light for a sight of land, so eager was he to reach his goal.

Soon after dawn they sighted the sandy coast of Pylos, and as they came closer in, they could see a great crowd of people gathered on the shore. For it was a holiday in honour of the great Poseidon, god of the seas, and all the townsfolk of Pylos had come together to offer sacrifice and do him homage. There were in all nine companies of them, with five hundred men in each; and each company was making its own sacrifices and offering up its particular prayers.

One company, consisting of the most noble men of Pylos, was led by the king, old Nestor himself, renowned throughout all Greece for his wisdom and discernment. He was now very old, but his understanding and true judgement were as they had always been, and he was yet respected far and wide. Though he had been old already when the Greeks had sailed for Troy, almost twenty years before, he had sailed with them, along with his eldest son, and the Grecian host had found his prudent counsel of the greatest service. But he had returned alone from Troy, for his son, Antilochus, had perished in the fighting, and his spirit had been among those Odysseus had seen in Hades' land.

As the young men from Ithaca rowed in to the shore a little way along the coast from where the people were gathered, the sacrifices had been done and the folk were building fires and spreading rugs upon the ground that they might sit and feast. Busily and gaily they unpacked baskets of food and broke open jars of wine, setting out the good things on the coloured cloths. They were all in festive holiday attire, garlanded and with their brightest garments, and made a cheerful sight to greet Telemachus as he stepped out on the beach.

But he was a little fearful of how he might approach the king before all this vast concourse, and stood hesitating by the little ship, for it was the very first time in all his nineteen years that he had gone to visit a man of such importance as wise King Nestor.

But one of Nestor's youngest sons, Peisistratus, who had long since spied the ship when she was but a white sail on the horizon, had kept a careful watch on her as she drew close in to the shore; and now, as soon as he saw Telemachus set foot upon the golden sand, he came forward to the water's edge to welcome him.

Telemachus looked up to see a youth of his own age coming towards him with a smile, and he recovered his spirits and smiled in return. Peisistratus held out his hand. 'You are welcome, stranger,' he said cordially, 'we men of Pylos are about to start the feasting, come and join us.' He led the way back to the group that he had left. 'My father is King Nestor,' he said. 'I will take you to him, for he is ever glad to receive a stranger.'

As Telemachus came among them, many of the men of Pylos greeted him with friendliness, and by the time he stood before the king, he was once again at ease. Nestor sat upon a heap of fleecy sheepskins talking with his sons.

'Here is the stranger who has just moored his ship a little way along the coast, father,' said Peisistratus.

Nestor looked up at Telemachus, and the eyes in his wrinkled face were very bright and keen. He smiled, 'Come and sit close beside me, young man, and eat and drink with us. Afterwards we will talk together, and you shall tell me who you are and from whence you come.'

They ate barley cakes and meat that had been roasted on spits over the fire, and out of the golden cups from the king's own house, which had been carried to the shore wrapped in linen and laid in a wooden chest, they drank wine to the long life and good health of Nestor and his sons, and fair weather to prosper the voyaging of Telemachus.

When they had eaten and drunk, Nestor turned to Telemachus. 'Stranger,' he said, 'now that you have been welcomed among us with food and wine, it is a fitting time to ask you your name and your country. Do you voyage to a destination, or is the sea your home?'

'Good Nestor, I am not a sea-robber, if that is what you mean, for my home is in Ithaca. And I voyage to a destination which I have even now reached. For it is you, most noble king, whom I have travelled over the sea to seek. My name is Telemachus, and I am the only son of Odysseus, king of Ithaca. But it is not on behalf of my father's people that I have come to you, it is to ask your aid for my own self. I have come to question you if you have heard news of Odysseus since he sailed from Troy. You were in that city with him when it fell, perchance you may have sailed for home together, and then been parted on the way, or perchance you may have heard from another's lips of some mishap that has befallen him. For you must know that though it is near to ten whole years since Troy was taken, my father has not yet returned to Ithaca. Good Nestor, if you know anything of him, tell me now, and tell me truly. Do not seek to spare me if your news is bad, for I would rather learn the worst there is to know, than live on longer in this uncertainty, ever wondering whether my father really will come home again or whether he is lost to me and to my mother for evermore.'

Nestor laid a hand on Telemachus' shoulder. 'Truly,' he said, 'I should have known you, for you are very like your father. May you as much resemble him in courage and resourcefulness as you do in looks.' He nodded his head thoughtfully, and smiled. 'Good Odysseus, well do I remember his cautious counsel and his cunning wiles, no man of all the Greeks was like him; never-despairing through all those dark days of war and composed in the time of victory. For those were unhappy years for us, as all years of war must be, when before Troy perished so many goodly leaders of the Greeks. On Trojan earth fell Achilles, beautiful and so young, and brave Patroclus, his friend. There, too, died Antilochus, my son. Indeed they were unhappy years, Telemachus. But of the number who were slain, your father was not one, for when the city was taken, he sailed for Ithaca with his twelve ships. More than that I cannot tell you, for when the time came for the Greeks to set sail for home, a quarrel arose between Agamemnon, our leader, and his brother Menelaus, king of Sparta. One was for doing one thing and the other was for doing another, and between their two opposing counsels the whole Greek host was divided. I was among those who agreed with Menelaus, and we set sail together, but your father turned back while out at sea, returned to land, and stayed to follow Agamemnon. Thus have I no tidings of Odysseus, whether he set sail again and perished on the sea, or whether he is even now wandering about the world, ever striving to reach his home. For in the years that have passed since I myself reached Pylos, I have heard from travellers news of one or other of the Greeks who fought at Troy, but there has been no word of Odysseus, your father.'

'Good Nestor,' said Telemachus, 'I thank you for what you have told me, little comfort though it brings me. For I fear that if my father comes not soon, he will find no home left to him, no possessions to call his own, and his land and his servants given to another.' And Telemachus told King Nestor of the suitors and how they wasted Odysseus' goods, and of their overbearing ways and their insolence to him.

Solemnly, old Nestor shook his head. 'It is indeed a grievous thing, that in the master's absence such things can come to pass within his house. I would for your sake, good Telemachus, that the day may not be far distant which sees Odysseus return to his home.'

'Though I long every minute for that to come to pass,' said Telemachus, 'yet of late have I grown afraid that day will never come, and that my father's bones are even now lying in an alien grave, or washed beneath the restless sea.' He sighed. 'But this is no fit way for a guest to talk who has been so kindly received, and on a day which should be a day of rejoicing and holiday for his hosts. Good King Nestor, let us talk of other things than of my troubles. Tell me instead tales of the other leaders of the Greeks, for you have known them all, and in your wisdom judged them all aright, and can tell me truly what manner of men they were.'

And so they sat, and Nestor talked all through the afternoon of Agamemnon, Menelaus, and the other mighty

men, while Telemachus listened eagerly to all he had to say. And the sun went down while Nestor talked, and he looked up at the sunset-colours of the sky. 'I have talked enough for one day,' he said, 'and you have listened very patiently, but before we rise and leave this place, there is one thing that I would tell you. Stay not long away from your home, my child, lest those suitors of your mother begin to plot fresh mischief. But before you return to Ithaca, I would urge you to go to Sparta and talk to Menelaus. For he has but lately returned to his own home after many wanderings and much delay in foreign lands, and it may well be that he has tidings of your father. If you would travel to Sparta over land, and that is surely the best way, then shall I willingly lend you horses, and one of my sons shall be your guide.'

Telemachus thanked him; and after one last cup of wine had been poured and drunk, the men of Pylos rose to pack away their rugs and cups and platters in chests and baskets for carrying home. Telemachus would have gone to the ship to pass the night on board with the young men who had come with him, but Nestor would not permit this, saying, 'No guest shall ever be turned away from any house of mine while there are blankets and rugs to spare. And never shall the son of my good friend Odysseus say that Nestor left him to sleep upon a ship moored on the beach at Pylos.'

So Telemachus went with Nestor and his sons to their house, and after they had feasted they went to rest; and for Telemachus a bed was set in the guest-chamber in the vestibule, and young Peisistratus slept with him for company.

In the morning Nestor sacrificed to Athene a pure white

heifer, garlanded with flowers, and with gilded horns, that she might look with favour on the mission of Telemachus. And after the sacrifice they feasted, King Nestor and his family together with Telemachus and his young companions from Noemon's ship.

When the feasting was done, Nestor called to his sons to bring out his finest travelling chariot and yoke to it his fastest horses, for Telemachus to drive to Sparta with Peisistratus. Then, after they had said farewell, and Nestor and his elder sons had wished Telemachus god-speed, Peisistratus took up the reins and they set off at a good pace across the level land that led to Sparta.

To Telemachus the drive was strange and exciting, and he envied Peisistratus his skill in driving. For Ithaca had steep and rocky ways and narrow roads where driving was impossible, so there were but few horses on the island.

They drove all day, and spent the night half-way to Sparta in the house of a kindly host; and early in the morning they set off once more. By the afternoon they had reached the wide lands of Menelaus, driving through the valleys past his cornfields with the young green wheat, and the fields of sprouting barley where the little yellow-eyed red tulips grew; and at dusk they came in sight of the high roofs of his palace in hill-encircled Sparta.

XI

Menelaus and Helen

IN his splendid palace great King Menelaus was celebrating with a banquet the betrothal of his daughter, Hermione, Queen Helen's only child, to young Neoptolemus, Achilles' son, whom Odysseus had seen acquit himself so bravely in the wooden horse at Troy. For while they fought side by side, Menelaus had promised Neoptolemus that one day he should marry his fair daughter; and he was even now making good his word, and after days of feasting and rejoicing, Hermione would be sent from Sparta with an escort of many chariots to the land of the Myrmidons where her bridegroom ruled and waited for her to come to him.

With singing and with music and with the antics of two acrobatic jugglers, King Menelaus entertained his guests.

The minstrel played upon his lyre and sang a song that was fitting for a betrothal feast, while to the music the acrobats danced in and out among the feasters, walking on their hands, leaping over each other's back, and whirling on hands and feet like wheels down the length of the great hall; and much applause and praise they got for their skilled performance.

While the banquet was in progress, Telemachus and Peisistratus arrived at the palace and were received by Menelaus' steward who left them waiting in the courtyard, while he went to ask his master what he desired should be done with the strangers. 'Shall I bring them here to you, or shall I send them on to find hospitality in another house, my lord?'

Menelaus smashed his clenched fist down upon the carved arm of his chair. 'Why, man, you are a fool even to think of asking me such a question,' he roared. 'Have I ever turned away a guest? Do I not always welcome all strangers in my house? Go at once and bring them in.' The steward turned and hurried off and Menelaus gave a good-humoured chuckle. 'The man is growing crazed in his wits,' he said. 'He knows he does not need to ask a thing like that.' He took a draught of wine. 'These strangers come at a timely moment, the more guests at a betrothal feast, the merrier for the feasters. Come, my friends, do not stint the wine.'

Menelaus was a big man with a loud voice and a jovial laugh and a sandy beard streaked with grey, and a kindly heart which even his rough manner could not hide. He greeted Telemachus and Peisistratus warmly and called to them, 'Sit down, young men, and eat and drink and make merry with us. And later you can tell me who you are and whence you come, for I can see at a single glance that you are nobly born. No peasant breeds such sons as you. Come, sit and eat, there is food and wine in plenty in this house.'

Telemachus gazed in admiration and wonder at the splendour of the great hall of Menelaus, for Menelaus was a rich and mighty king and his house well displayed his wealth. To Telemachus it seemed most wonderful that any mortal man should own such glory and magnificence. For in all his life he had seen nothing comparable and had never been so far from home, or indeed travelled farther from Ithaca than the islands which lay close by. And though Odysseus had been a prince much respected among the Greeks, Ithaca was only a small land, and a poor one when compared with the hills and vales of Sparta, and Odysseus' house seemed but simple beside the lofty palace of King Menelaus.

With astonishment Telemachus saw the walls inlaid with bronze and gold and silver, and set with amber and with ivory designs; and marvelled at the ornaments and furnishings. He leant across to Peisistratus and whispered, 'Look well, Peisistratus, at all this pomp around us. I have never seen the like before. Surely not even the immortal gods themselves have so much splendour on high Olympus.'

But Menelaus heard his words and said, 'Come, good youths, you must not compare my possessions with the gods', it is not seemly. For the home and riches of the gods are everlasting, while mine must surely perish and one day fall to dust.' Then he smiled and looked around the hall with satisfaction. 'But though my goods are in no way comparable to those of the immortal gods, yet am I counted rich among men, and well may that be so, for I have gathered much wealth from many corners of the world, far-off lands and places where strange creatures dwell, and many curious sights have I seen in all my travels. The Egyptians with their rare, healing drugs; and the Ethiopians who are black; and, if you can believe it, in Libya lambs which are born with horns, not once, but three times a year, so that to the Libyans there is a never-failing supply of woolly fleeces and fresh ewes' milk cheese. But if I were to tell you one part of all that I have seen, I should talk until the dawn.' He drank a cup of wine and sighed. 'Yet all my riches do not avail to keep away the sorrow that comes upon me when I remember the many friends of mine who fought with me, and died at Troy. I would give up my wealth willingly if it could bring them back from among the dead, for they were fine men and good companions.' He paused a moment, then went on, 'But of all those who are dead and gone, I think I mourn not any so much as brave Odysseus of Ithaca, for I considered him the best of all the Greeks. Yet do I not know today whether he is alive or dead, for ten years after Troy has fallen he is still not returned to his home. Truly, if I do grieve so much for him, who was my friend, how much more must he be lamented by his father, old Laertes, and by good Penelope, his wife, and by Telemachus, his only son, who was but a tiny child when his father sailed for Troy. Indeed, poor souls, I do pity them.'

Telemachus' eyes filled with tears when he heard his father talked of, and he turned away his head so that Menelaus might not see him weep. But Menelaus marked him, and even as he wondered what there should have been in his words to make a young man weep who was not old enough to have known Odysseus and to have been his friend, he saw the likeness of Telemachus to his father.

'That is Odysseus' son,' he thought to himself. 'It can be no other.' And he weighed in his mind whether to ask him outright if he were his old friend's son, or to wait until the youth spoke himself. 'It were perhaps best to wait,' he thought. 'I do not wish to grieve him more. He will tell me his name in his own good time.'

He was about to speak of other and more happy matters, when his wife, Queen Helen, accompanied by three of her maids, came into the great hall. The guests greeted her with courtesy, and quietly and graciously she answered them, taking her place near Menelaus, seemingly intent upon receiving from her serving-maids the spinning they had carried for her. Yet had her swift eyes seen the two strangers present, and marked the likeness of one of the youths to Odysseus, though she had but glanced at him for a single moment.

On their part, Telemachus and Peisistratus watched her with curiosity, for was she not Helen for whose sake the Greeks had fought at Troy, accounting their sufferings a privilege? Helen, said once to be the most beautiful woman in all the world; who, twenty years before, had slipped away from this very hall, and sailed to Troy with King Priam's son, leaving her husband, Menelaus. Yet because she was beautiful, and because these things are as the gods will them to be, no one blamed her for the sorrow she had caused.

The two young men watched her as she took up her golden distaff and moved her shapely hands among the violet wool, and though one of them had had a brother who had died at Troy, and the other mourned a father, whom, because of her, he might never see again, they knew that Helen was still blameless and still worth dying for; and that though twenty years had passed since that fatal day when she had left her home, she was still the loveliest woman in all the world.

Helen laid a hank of purple yarn in her silver work-basket which ran on little wheels, and as though she knew they had been watching her, looked up with a smile at Telemachus and Nestor's son, before turning to her husband. 'Do you know, Menelaus,' she asked in her sweet, low voice, 'who these strangers are? Have you asked their names?'

Menelaus replied, 'They have but now arrived within our walls, and I have not harassed them with questions, hoping that when they had feasted, they would feel inclined to talk and tell their names and country.'

Helen smiled again and went on, 'Never in my life have I seen so great a likeness to another man as in the resemblance of this youth to Odysseus. I am certain that this is no other than Telemachus, Odysseus' son, whom he left as a tiny babe when he sailed to Troy with you.'

Delighted that he too had guessed the same, Menelaus said, 'Truly, that is the very thought that had been also in my mind, that this is Odysseus' son. He has Odysseus' features, his very gestures and the movement of his eyes. I surely could not be mistaken.' And he looked inquiringly towards Telemachus, who suddenly felt very young and very shy in all the distinguished company, and very much afraid that his quest might prove unpleasing to his host.

But Peisistratus came to his aid and answered for him. 'You are right, King Menelaus, you and your noble queen, this is indeed Telemachus, the son of Odysseus and his wife Penelope, who has travelled from rocky Ithaca to speak with you. For a son is lonely when he has no father to advise him. My own father, Nestor, king of Pylos, has sent me with him to guide him on the way, since he is unfamiliar with the mainland.'

'Glad am I to welcome to my house the son of my dear friend Odysseus,' said Menelaus. 'But indeed, I should be gladder if I might see his father here with him tonight. While I fought at Troy I often thought, how when the war was over and Odysseus and I were returned to Greece, I should give him to rule over, one of the towns of Argos, near to my own Sparta. There he could have lived with his family and all his people, so that we might have often met, remaining firm friends until the day death parted us. But although I returned safely to my house, notwithstanding after much toil, fate has been hard to great Odysseus, and denied to him his joyous homecoming.'

At his words a deep sadness fell upon the gathering, and many wept; for dear ones they had lost, or for troubles of their own, or just for the unhappiness of man, who lives not only to rejoice, but to suffer also.

Then Peisistratus spoke, 'Noble Menelaus, it is right that we should mourn for those who have died before us, it is indeed the only gift we can offer to the dead, our poor unavailing tears. But this is a festive occasion, the betrothal of your fair daughter, Queen Helen's child, so let us not mar it with grief for things we cannot alter even by our weeping.'

'Old Nestor has ever been famed for his wisdom,' said

Menelaus, 'and it is plain to see that in this respect, at least, you, his son, resemble him. You are right, Peisistratus, let us have no more of grief. Come, fill up the cups with wine again and we will drink to happier days.'

Then spoke Helen, with all the quick perception that was hers, 'Dear husband, and all you noble guests of ours, why do we not tell tales to while away the time? For there is no way by which we mortals can so forget our ills, as in the telling and the hearing of stories of brave deeds and stirring times.'

Many were the voices raised in accord, and Menelaus said, 'That was well thought and well spoken, Helen. Let you be the first to tell a tale, for I know of no one more skilled than you in relating a good story.'

With her eyes now on the wool she spun, now swiftly passing over the company with a smile of charm and sweetness, in her low, clear voice Helen began, 'Since it is the noble King Odysseus whom we have foremost in our hearts tonight, the story that I shall tell you is of him. I cannot relate to you all the perils and the hardships he endured so bravely when he was fighting with his comrades, for I was not there, but I can tell you one tale about him which only I recall. You all have heard of his resourcefulness and cunning, how he was pre-eminent in subtle ways and means, and how an artful contrivance was to him the chiefest joy of life. Once, during the siege, seeking for some way of gaining knowledge of how things went within the Trojan walls, it came to his mind to disguise himself as a beggar, and in this humble dissemblance to wander through the city, watching carefully all that he could see. In dirty rags and hungering, his body bruised and tired—even so well had he disguised himself—he came to the city gates and was passed through. As a beggar he asked for alms in the street, and thus continued for several days, always noting things that might have been of value to the Greeks. It was then that I saw and knew him, and that in spite of the dirty rags and his thin ribs showing through them. For of all in Troy, I alone had not only seen him from the city walls at a distance in his armour on the battlefield, but also close at hand as a guest in my husband's palace, here in Sparta, in the olden days. So I asked him to my house under pretence of offering him my bounty, and he came willingly, for he thought that I might know the counsels of the Trojan king. I called him Odysseus, and tried to trick him by every means I had into admitting that he was the man I knew him to be. But all my skilful wiles he countered with his own, and at last I saw that he had won, and that I could never trap him into discovering himself. So I swore a great oath not to betray him to the Trojans, and he laughed and said, "Truly, Helen, there is no deceiving you, I am indeed Odysseus, as you well do know."

'After that we talked long together. He told me of the plans of the Grecian army and asked me many questions about the Trojans, and every one of them I answered truthfully, for of all the women within the walls of Troy, my heart alone was with the Greeks. For I was even then repenting of my rash folly, and longing to see once more my home and Menelaus, my dear lord.'

'Why yes,' said Menelaus, when she had done, 'I well remember the many wiles and ruses of Odysseus. I have known and watched many warriors and many men of thought and counsel, but never have I found combined in one man the qualities of both, save in Odysseus.' And he smiled happily as he recollected the many tricks of his old friend.

And Telemachus felt a glow of pride burning in his heart, and he thought, 'Even if it is never given to me to see him, at least my father will have lived for me in the good words and in the praise of other men.'

Menelaus chuckled. 'And what a fine thing it was he did when all we leaders of the Greeks lay hidden in the wooden horse,' he said. 'It was his wisdom and his craft that saved us then. It was when the hollow wooden horse, with all us warriors hid inside, had been dragged within the city walls by the men of Troy. There we waited in the stifling darkness until night should fall, ever wondering if at any moment the Trojans would regret their action in receiving in their midst the wooden horse, and begin to batter it to pieces, and find and slaughter us like helpless children, one by one, or to lay beneath it burning fire and char us all to ashes. It was then—do you remember, Helen?—you came to the assembly place with Prince Deiphobus, old King Priam's son, to look upon the horse. Three times you walked around it, sounding with your knuckles its hollow sides, and we waited in terror within, almost not daring to breathe, while we wondered if our secret had been guessed. As indeed it had; but the immortal gods were good to us and it was only you who suspected that there were men hidden inside the horse. And after that you called to us, the leaders of the Greeks; you called to us every one by name, crying out the name of each man in the voice of his beloved wife. So that in the darkness each of us in turn leapt to his feet and would have answered you, believing that it was indeed his wife who called upon him, but that Odysseus guessed the trap at once and bade us in a whisper give no reply. Not even, Helen, when you spoke to him himself, and he heard from beyond the wooden wall, a voice that was even as the voice of his own dear Queen Penelope, pleading with him tearfully to speak with her, did he for one second falter. And as one after another, the false voices called to us by name, he would not let us answer, and one by one we were at last persuaded by his wisdom. All but Anticlus, and he, the obstinate one, would not believe Odysseus, and whispered to him, "You are a fool, Odysseus, not to recognize your own wife's voice. I swear that if I heard my wife speak to me so, I should answer her."

'And when he heard what he thought to be the voice of his wife, he started up and made to call to her, and so would we all have been destroyed, but that Odysseus, quick and crafty as ever, laid his hand upon the mouth of Anticlus and held it there until once again there was silence from without. Thus did Odysseus save us all, the leaders of the Greeks.'

'That is a noble story,' said Peisistratus. 'A tale worthy to be remembered and told many times.'

'Yet did all my father's wisdom and his guile in no way help him to avoid whatever fate it was that overtook him,' said Telemachus sadly. 'All his craft and all his cunning have not saved him nor brought him home to Ithaca.' He sighed. 'And now, great Menelaus, I beg of you that you will keep me here talking no longer, but instead let me lie down and rest, for I have heard much today that has moved me greatly, and I would think over in quiet all that you have said to me of my father, before I close my eyes in peaceful sleep.'

Helen ordered the servants to set up two beds in the guest-chamber for the visitors and spread them with warm blankets; and Menelaus bade all his other guests good night and they went to their homes in the town of Sparta. Then with many wishes for their comfort and sweet sleep, Telemachus and Peisistratus were lighted to their beds.

But in spite of their weariness, and in spite of the many thoughts that sped round in Telemachus' mind and his wish for quiet rest, the two youths could not refrain from talking long of all the wonders they had seen in the palace of Menelaus; his golden walls, his ivory-inlaid chairs, his embroidered hangings, the graceful acrobats; and Queen Helen, the loveliest woman in the world, for whose sake a city had been burnt.

XII

The Old Man of the Sea

VERY early in the morning Menelaus went to Telemachus, and finding him alone, sat down beside him, and without any hesitation, spoke his thoughts. 'Why have you come here, Telemachus?' he asked. 'For I do not believe that you have journeyed all the way from Ithaca to Sparta just to look at me and Helen, and compliment us on our lordly house. I think you had another purpose in your mind. What is it, young man? Come, tell me.'

'Great Menelaus,' replied Telemachus, 'you are right indeed. My reason for coming here was to ask you if you had any tidings of my father. For I am sore beset at home by the suitors of my mother, since they lay waste our house and our possessions. If my father returns not soon, we shall be ruined utterly.' And he told Menelaus of the suitors' greed and insolence; and of how he had called the people of Ithaca to an assembly, and how he had slipped forth from his home by night to sail to Pylos and to Sparta that he might seek for news of Odysseus. 'And now I beg you,' he said, 'if ever you loved Odysseus and wished him well—and if you spoke truly last night, you must indeed have done so—tell me the truth about him. If you have heard that he is dead, do not conceal the sorrow from me with kindly intentions, or if you have learnt that he is lost upon the wide sea or in some far-off land, then tell me all you know, King Menelaus, hiding nothing from me. For I am well-nigh desperate and I must know the truth, whether I can still hope for my father's return or not.'

When he had ceased, Menelaus exclaimed indignantly, 'The shameless rogues, to plague a good man's wife so in her husband's absence, and to devour his food and wine like vultures. I warrant that were you older, but few of them would dare to show their faces in Odysseus' house. It is indeed a sorry thing when young men can act in such a fashion, and I will not pity them, no, not I, when vengeance falls upon them. For a sad day will it be for them, the day Odysseus comes home once more and drives them forth with slaughter.'

'It will be a sad day for them, Menelaus, and a great day of rejoicing for me and my unhappy mother. But when that day will come, or whether I do merely hope for it in vain, are the questions I have come to ask of you. Good Menelaus, have you any tidings of my father?'

'Would that I could give you comforting news, but I have none to offer you.' Menelaus shook his head. 'No, none. Since we set sail from Troy, I with certain other leaders of the Greeks, and Odysseus to follow my brother Agamemnon whither he would lead him, I have heard but once of your good father, how he fared, and that was from Proteus, the Old Man of the Sea.'

'What news did Proteus give you?' asked Telemachus eagerly.

'But little, I fear, Telemachus, yet I will tell it to you. Sailing home from Troy my ships were becalmed on an island off the coast of Egypt. There we waited, day after day, for a wind to speed us back to Sparta. But for twenty days never a breeze blew heavier than a man could breathe. The supplies were finished and my men were in despair, and I do not know how it would have ended, had not the sea-nymph Eidothea looked up through the blue water and seen and pitied me. To me she came as I walked alone along the shore, rising up out of the sea, all wet, and with a crown of seaweed on her dripping hair. She spoke to me in a voice that was like the crying of a seagull as it flies inland on a windy day. "Stranger, why do you tarry here upon this isle?"

'"Because the sea is calm and flat, and there is no wind for me to sail by," I answered her. "I fear that in some way I must have displeased the gods, that they make no wind to blow to carry me over the water to my home. But," I went on, "if you, gracious goddess, whoever you may be, could give me your blessing and your help, then might my men be saved from starving and we might leave this island."

'She answered me in that same strange, melancholy voice, harshly musical, "I am Eidothea, daughter of Proteus, the Old Man of the Sea, who serves the god Poseidon and who knows all the oceans as you know the rooms of your own house. I cannot tell you wherein you have offended the immortal gods, or what you should do to leave this place, yet my father Proteus could tell you. But you must lie in wait for him and catch him and hold him fast before you ask your questions, or he will not stay to answer them. If you lay hold of him, he will be bound to answer any question that you put to him; when you will see again your home and in what manner; and, if you should wish to know, all that has happened in your house since you left it, long ago. But Proteus will not be easily caught, and being caught, not easily held, so you will need much strength and skill and other men to help you."

'This seemed to me to be but poor advice, that I should lay hold of an immortal being from the sea, who was hard to catch and harder still to hold, and who most probably dwelt in the blue depths of the water where no man might venture. So I said to her, "Tell me then, of your kindness, some way that I may take your father, some trap which I may prepare for him, and where he may be found. For alone, without your enchantments for my help, could I accomplish nothing of all you bid me."

'Instantly she answered, promising me her aid. "Every day," she said, "at the time when the sun is highest in the sky, the Old Man of the Sea rises up out of the blue water with his myriad seals, like a shepherd with his flock. And he lies down to sleep among them in the heat of the afternoon, all of them together, lying in slumber upon the sand. If you would capture my father, early in the morning you must hide yourself on the beach with three of your men and lie in wait until he comes with all his seals. First will he count each one, and then lie down to sleep, and at that moment you and your companions must rise up and take hold of him. In spite of all his struggles you must not let him go, and do not be deterred by the strange shapes he will take. For he will turn himself into all manner of beasts, and into fire and water, in his crafty efforts to escape. But you must remember, that whatever fearful shape he takes, you must not fail to hold him fast. For if you once let him go, he will be lost to you, and you will have no chance to speak with him again. But when at last you see him as himself once more, then may you release him, and he will answer all your questions truly." And with that the strange sea-nymph dived back into the water.

'I returned to my ships thinking over all that she had said to me, and in the morning I chose out three of my companions, good men all, whom I thought best fitted for the adventure, and together we went to the place where, the day before, I had seen Eidothea. We had not been there above a moment, when she came to us, up through the sea, bearing with her the skins of four seals. She led us to the spot where every day her father came to sleep, and there she showed us how to hollow out in the sand four hiding-places; and when we had lain down in them, she covered us with the skins. And I can tell you, Telemachus, that those skins smelt most unbearably of fish, but thoughtful Eidothea had brought with her ambrosia, such as the gods alone may eat, and a particle of this she placed beneath the nose of each one of us. And so sweet was the fragrance of the ambrosia to our mortal senses, that all the while we lay in wait for Proteus, we could smell nothing else.

'Then Eidothea left us to watch and wait alone, and

exactly at midday the seals came up out of the blue water and lay down upon the shore to bask in the hot sun. They lay all around us, thinking from the skins with which we were covered that we too were seals. And lastly came old Proteus himself. And if his daughter was strange to look upon, the Old Man of the Sea was a great deal stranger, of that I can assure you. First, as Eidothea had told me that he would, he counted all his seals, and never suspecting the trap that we had laid for him, he counted us among their number. Then he too lay down to sleep upon the sand.

'As soon as we judged that he was fast asleep, we crept quietly upon him and laid hold of him, all of us together, with a mighty shout. At once he awoke and struggled, and when he found that he could not free himself, then did he begin to take the shapes of other things, even as Eidothea had warned me. First he became a lion with a shaggy mane, roaring most terribly. Then he was a huge snake, hissing and writhing in our hands and ever striving to slip from our grasp. After that he turned himself into a spotted leopard which growled and bit and tore at our hands with long curved claws. And then he took the form of a great boar, fierce and snorting, with mighty tusks. After that, perhaps most difficult of all, he lost his shape and melted into water, which would have trickled through the sand and been lost, had we not all held a few drops of it in our cupped hands. Then suddenly he became a tall tree, with a broad trunk and wide leafy branches, growing higher every moment as though it would outreach our grasp.

'But in spite of all these bewildering changes, we held on to him, and at last he became wearied of the struggle, and taking once more his own shape, he said, "I doubt not but

that one of the immortals told you how I might be overcome, you bold men, or else should I have escaped easily from you. But what is it that you would ask of me?"

'At once I spoke up and told him what I longed to know, and he answered me, "The gods are angered with you, for you forgot to make them fit offerings before setting sail for home from Troy. And truly, until those offerings are made, you will never see your own land. You must return to Egypt first and there pay to the immortal gods those sacrifices you have neglected. Then only will you find a favourable wind to bear you quickly over the sea to Sparta."

'I can tell you, Telemachus, my heart was heavy to hear his words, that I had to return to Egypt and meet with more delays. But I thought that while I had before me the Old Man of the Sea who knew the answers to all questions, I should be foolish if I did not ask him further concerning the matters which were dear to me. So I questioned him about the other leaders of the Greeks, whether they had reached their homes safely, or if any had perished on the waves. And old Proteus told me truly about all that I asked, for in every case except your father's, I heard later that all these things had come to pass, just as he said. But of what he said about Odysseus, I have yet no way of finding if it were the truth.

'But this is what he said to me of your father. "Odysseus, king of Ithaca, is alive and has not perished in the sea, though all his ships and all his men are lost to him. He alone of all the men of Ithaca who fought at Troy, still lives, but in great sorrow. For the immortal nymph Calypso keeps him in her toils, a prisoner on her island of Ogygia."

'After that I had no heart to ask him further, and he

dived down into the sea, and all his seals went with him, a mighty herd. And the next morning we rowed back to Egypt, and there offered sacrifice to the immortal gods, as he had said. And they were appeased and sent us a fair wind, and we sailed with all speed to Sparta. But that is indeed all that I have learnt of good Odysseus since he set out from Troy, that he is not dead, but the captive of a fair immortal nymph.'

Telemachus sighed deeply. 'There is comfort in that my father still lives,' he said, 'but his plight brings me to despair. My mother has ever told me, and I have heard, too, from many other lips, of my father's famed cunning and resourcefulness. But how can even the most wily of all men break free from the bonds of an immortal?'

Menelaus laid a hand upon his shoulder. 'You know that I wish my news had been more consoling, but, good youth, you must never give up hope, Odysseus may yet come home. Meanwhile, you are welcome in my house for as long as you care to stay. And when you wish to return to Ithaca, I will see that it is well laden with gifts that you go. Among other things that I should like to see you call your own, I have a mind to give you three of my finest horses, pure white, with flowing manes and tails, and a swift chariot, for I think that you have nothing comparable to them at home.'

'King Menelaus,' replied Telemachus, 'I thank you with all my heart. And I am telling you the truth when I say to you that gladly would I spend whole months with you in Sparta, listening to your tales and hearing of my father's deeds. But the good comrades who sailed with me to Pylos will already be impatient for my return, and kind Noemon, who lent his ship to me, may soon have need of her, so I must not tarry many days. For your gifts I thank you, they will be truly welcome, but please, great Menelaus, give me no horses. For Ithaca is a rough and rocky land, with narrow roads and stony tracks and no wide paths suitable for driving on. That indeed is why at home we have no horses. Though I am grateful for your thoughtfulness,' he went on seriously, 'I would rather that you kept your horses, for here in Sparta the ways are broad and you have wide fields and pasture-lands, good ground for swift and noble steeds.'

Menelaus gave a mighty chuckle and clapped him on the shoulder. 'You shall go without your horses, I promise you,' he said. 'But I will see that old Nestor's chariot is well filled with other gifts for you to stow on board your borrowed ship. Gold cups and mixing-bowls and dishes and such like. Things that will be acceptable and useful even in little rugged Ithaca.'

And they looked at one another and both laughed together.

XIII

Telemachus returns to Ithaca

BUT at the very moment when Telemachus, in Menelaus' palace, was talking with his jovial host, in the house of Odysseus the suitors were competing with each other at throwing the javelin in the courtyard. And Antinous and Eurymachus stood out among the others for their skill, and showed themselves the wooers' acknowledged leaders in games as in all else.

While they amused themselves thus, up from the town to Odysseus' house, came friendly Noemon, who had lent Telemachus his ship. Telemachus had been gone from home longer than the kindly man had expected, and he was even now in need of his ship, for he wished to sail to Elis on the mainland, where he had a young mule he wanted to break in. He stood at the gates looking around the courtyard and saw no sign of Telemachus, as indeed he had not thought to do, for he knew that had the youth returned, he would at once have come to him in the town and told him that his ship was back, for it was not like Telemachus to be careless and neglectful with a friend.

Catching sight of Antinous, Noemon went over to him, and greeting him, asked, 'Do you know, Antinous, when Telemachus will return from Pylos? He borrowed my ship for the journey, and now I need her to sail to the pastures of Elis, where I keep my mules.'

The suitors were astonished when they heard his question, for they had not thought Telemachus had gone to Pylos as he had vowed he would. 'It is true we have not seen him for several days,' they whispered to each other, 'but it seemed most likely that he was sulking in his room because we laughed at him, or that he had gone to visit his grandfather, old Lord Laertes, on his farm, or that he was with his swineherd or his cowman, counting over his pigs and cattle, to see how many we have eaten.'

Antinous frowned in anger, and with difficulty controlled his rage. 'I did not know our host had gone to Pylos,' he said as pleasantly as he could. 'Tell me all you know of this voyage of his, Noemon. Was he accompanied by slaves, or did he persuade some of the young men of Ithaca to go with him? And did you willingly lend him your ship, or did he, in the name of his father the king, take her from you against your wishes?'

'Why no, Antinous,' replied Noemon, 'I lent her to him willingly. What else could I have done? The good youth seemed so eager for a ship, pleading with tears in his eyes that I would lend him mine. He has taken with him about twenty companions, young lads like himself, all still boys enough to enjoy the sail to Pylos as though it were an adventure.'

Antinous' frown grew blacker and his fingers tightened on the javelin he held, but he said nothing, though in his heart there were evil thoughts.

'Since you can in no way help me by telling me when he will return,' Noemon went on, 'there is small good in my remaining here to interrupt your sport. I will go back to my home now and sail to Elis another day. I have no doubt but that Telemachus will come to me the very moment that he lands to tell me of the arrival of my ship. Farewell to you all, noble wooers of our queen. May you enjoy your games.' And with that he went, walking back towards the town.

But Antinous and Eurymachus called the other suitors around them, and Antinous spoke to them all. 'My friends,' he said, 'Telemachus has won in this matter of the journey to Pylos. If this is the beginning of his new attitude towards us, then we had best take warning from it.' He paused a moment, and then said with evil meaning, 'My friends, would it not be a good thing for us if Telemachus did not return to Ithaca, but instead were, like his father, lost at sea?'

Many voices agreed with him, and others murmured, 'It would indeed be a happy day for us, for he has become a tedious critic of all we do and we should be well without him. Besides, with husband and with only son both lost to her, the queen would be forced to make up her mind to marry once again.'

Antinous looked at his companions. 'Give me a ship, and

let twenty of you come with me, and Telemachus will not return to Ithaca,' he said shortly. 'I will lie in wait for him in the narrow strait that lies between Ithaca and the isle of Same.'

The suitors one and all agreed to his proposal, and, well satisfied, he set himself to pick out his twenty comrades for the slaying, urging every one of the suitors to speak no word of what they proposed when they were within the house lest report of it should reach Penelope.

But Medon, Odysseus' faithful herald, had been sitting behind a pillar in the porch while they were at their games, resting himself, for he was no longer quite so young as he once had been, and he overheard all their plotting. Quickly and quietly and unseen he now slipped into the house and hurried to Penelope.

With old Eurycleia, the queen was sorting yarn for weaving, laying it away in baskets in careful skeins. She looked up and saw Medon coming. 'Have my suitors sent you, Medon,' she asked bitterly, 'to demand more entertainment from this unhappy, despoiled house? Truly, that is all you seem to do these days, to run errands for the wooers and request more food and wine from me for them.'

'No, good queen, though with all my heart I wish that today I had to come to you only to ask more food and wine for these wicked men. But it is no longer meat and drink alone that will content them. I heard them but even now plotting against the life of our dear prince. For it seems Telemachus has sailed to Pylos to seek tidings of his father, our lost king, and false Antinous with twenty more of the suitors is going to take a ship and ambush him as he returns to Ithaca.'

Dark despair fell upon Penelope when she heard his words, and for a while she could find no thoughts to speak. So, with a heavy heart, Medon left her quietly. At last she said, 'Why did no one tell me sooner that my son was gone to Pylos? Perhaps had I known of his intentions I might have persuaded him to stay at home. But he is gone, because you would not tell me, you cruel, faithless women, and now he will be killed.'

'Blame not the others, mistress,' said Eurycleia, 'for they knew not of what Telemachus proposed to do. To me alone he told all and made me swear a great oath not to tell you he was gone until at least twelve days had passed.'

'So has he gone to his own death,' sobbed Penelope. 'Nurse, what shall we do? Poor helpless women as we are with no menfolk to aid us.' In her despair she remembered Odysseus' father. 'Let us send to old Laertes on his farm, he will perhaps devise some plan which may yet save Telemachus from death.'

But Eurycleia thought of Telemachus' words, when he had told her, 'I think that one of the immortal gods is with me in this.' And she took Penelope in her arms to comfort her, and said, 'No, dear mistress, do not trouble further that good old noble lord, Laertes. He has grief enough of his own, and besides, what could he do to help? No, rather dry your eyes and cease those tears, and pray to the gods that they may see our Telemachus safely home. For with the gods, and with them alone, are all things possible.'

Penelope took the nurse's good advice, and going to her room, prayed to Athene, till, from weariness and worrying, she fell asleep. And while she slept she dreamt that she spoke with her sister, Iphthime, whom she had not seen for many years, for she lived far away. And Iphthime said to her, 'Fear not for your son, Penelope, for great Athene guards him well, and he will come back in safety to his home.' And in her sleep the queen was comforted.

But Antinous went with twenty others towards the shore, and setting sail in a small ship belonging to one of their number, they moored her in the harbour of a tiny isle half-way across the strait that lay between the islands of Ithaca and Same, and from there they kept a look-out for the ship which bore Telemachus.

That very same night, Athene appeared to Telemachus where he lay in the guest-chamber of Menelaus' palace. 'Come, Telemachus,' she bade him, 'make all haste home to Ithaca, for it is unwise of you to leave so long unwatched those suitors in your house. Who knows what mischief they may not do in your absence? Indeed, even now, with Antinous as their leader, twenty of them with a ship lie in wait for you in the strait between Ithaca and Same, with death in their hearts for you should your ship pass that way. But with speed sail home from Pylos, rowing day and night, and steer clear of the little isle that lies midway across the strait. When you reach Ithaca, go not at once to your father's house, but send instead your ship and your comrades to the town, and go yourself to the farm of Eumaeus the swineherd, who loves you well, and bid him take to your mother the message of your safe return.' With these words she vanished, and Telemachus jumped up, and going to the other bed, woke Peisistratus.

'Quickly, Peisistratus,' he exclaimed, 'we must leave this

place at once. The immortal Athene has just appeared to me to bid me hasten home.'

Peisistratus sat up in bed, rubbing his eyes. 'But, Telemachus,' he protested, 'it is yet dark. Not even that you have seen a goddess, will excuse our discourtesy in rousing Menelaus from his rest before the dawn to speed us on our way. What would he think of such inconsiderate guests?'

'But, Peisistratus, it is most urgent that I should go home.'

'Then you will have to go alone, and on foot,' replied Peisistratus firmly, 'for I cannot drive the horses in the dark, and you, remember, cannot drive a horse at all. So be patient for an hour or two.'

Telemachus saw the reasonableness of his friend's objections, and waited, though not patiently; and as early in the morning as he might without too much discourtesy, he went to Menelaus and asked that he might leave his house at once.

'I shall be sorry to see you go,' said Menelaus. 'But if you must, you must. Wait only until I have seen your gifts safely stowed in Nestor's chariot.' And he hurried off to choose fitting gifts for his two guests, and to order a meal to be prepared for them before they set off on their journey.

Among many other gifts from his treasure-house, Menelaus took a costly bowl of silver overlaid with gold, which had been given to him years before by the king of Sidon, who was famed for his wealth, and to Telemachus he said, 'This is indeed one of the most splendid of all my possessions, and gladly do I give it to you to take back to your home. Not only because you are the son of my dear friend

Odysseus, but for yourself alone, because you are a youth after my own heart.'

And Queen Helen chose out from her store of richly embroidered robes, packed away in chests of cedarwood, the finest and most lovely, worked in a many-coloured design of little flowers and olive leaves. So great indeed was the number of blossoms on it, that its wearer might well feel herself to be enwrapped in a fresh and fragrant meadow rather than in a garment. Taking it to Telemachus, Helen smiled at him and said, 'Give this robe to your mother to keep for you until the day you marry, and on that happy day may your young bride wear it, a gift from Helen, made by her own hands.'

When all the farewells had been said, Telemachus and Peisistratus took their places in the chariot and drove off at a fast pace across the lands of Sparta.

On the second day, when the town of Pylos came in sight, Telemachus said to Peisistratus, 'Good friend, if I ask a favour of you, will you do it for me?'

'Ask anything you want of me,' replied Peisistratus.

'Drive me down to my ship upon the shore at once, that I may embark today. Take me not first to your father, for that will cause me more delay. I do not wish to be discourteous to King Nestor, for I bear him a great respect, but the need is pressing that I should go home at once.'

Peisistratus sighed. 'My father will be angry with me if I do not bring you home with me. But, come, I will take you straightway to your ship, if that is your wish. For I would not have it said of me that I would not do a service for a friend.'

When they reached the shore, Telemachus found his

young companions waiting for him, and at once he bade them make ready to set sail.

'Go quickly, good Telemachus,' said Peisistratus. 'For if my father hears word that you are back in Pylos and about to leave for home, he will send for you with all speed, and there will be no refusing his invitation. I can assure you of that, for I know my father well.' With that he turned his horses' heads and drove the chariot towards the city and his father's palace.

'Make all the haste you can, my friends,' Telemachus urged the youths. 'We will not wait for a wind, but row to Ithaca.'

And led by Peiraeus, they ran to do his bidding, stowing away the tackle and Menelaus' costly gifts within the ship, and fitting the oars in their places.

Many of them were already on board, and Telemachus was on the point of giving the word to embark, when he saw a man coming towards him across the beach. The stranger had been walking quickly at first, but when he saw that the ship was about to put off to sea, he began to run, lest he should be too late to reach her. As soon as he was within hailing distance, he called to Telemachus and the other youths, 'Stay for me, good people, and I will be with you in a moment.' And at the command of Telemachus they waited for him while he ran over the sand.

When the man came up to them, recognizing Telemachus at once as the leader of the little group, he spoke to him, his breath coming in gasps, for he had been running fast. 'Good youth, are you leaving Pylos even now?'

'With all the speed that we may, stranger.'

'Whither are you bound?'

'To Ithaca, my home. My father is Odysseus, king of that island,' replied Telemachus, and then he added, 'Perhaps I should say Odysseus was my father, since he has not seen his home for twenty years, and I know not whether he still lives.'

The stranger said eagerly, 'Then I beg that you will take me with you. My name is Theoclymenus and my home was in Argos. But there, by mischance, did I slay a kinsman. His friends and brothers are searching for me and will kill me if they find me, and I believe that they have pursued me even to Pylos. If I can leave the mainland, and find sanctuary on one of the islands, it is most likely that they will not come after me, and I shall be safe. I pray you, let me sail to Ithaca with you.'

Telemachus hesitated and frowned a little, thinking, 'How can I offer hospitality to this stranger when in my father's house I have no authority? The suitors will insult him and maybe drive him forth. Because he is my guest and under my protection they will do this, since they have ever done all they can to slight me, and now are they eager even for my death. What safety can I offer to another man?'

Theoclymenus saw him frown and laid a hand upon his arm. 'I throw myself upon your mercy, good youth. Have pity on me.'

Telemachus looked at the stranger from Argos wondering what he should do, his young mind torn between two courses; on the one hand, to do nothing that would make more difficult and dangerous his own position in his father's house, and on the other, to help a man who was in peril of his life. He saw that Theoclymenus was young, not above thirty years, but his face was haggard and had grown old from weariness in no more than a few days, and there was fear in his eyes.

'Perhaps even so, at this very moment, my father pleads with some stranger in a far-off land, seeking safety from a foe,' said Telemachus to himself. 'What would I think of the man who could refuse him what he asks? Besides, were he in my place, here today, would he send away this man?' He looked again into the stranger's eyes and smiled and held out his hand. 'Come, Theoclymenus,' he said, 'but speedily, for I also am in haste to leave the shores of Pylos.'

They went on board together and the youths of Ithaca fell to rowing, and in a few moments, they were out at sea.

Theoclymenus sat by Telemachus in the stern of the ship and told him all his story. 'For generations,' he said, 'have my fathers been renowned throughout all Greece for their powers of prophecy. I also have this gift, which brought me honour and respect from men. But I quarrelled with a cousin at my home in Argos, and we fought together, and I killed him. His brothers are many and powerful in the land, and they and his friends have all sworn to slay me in revenge, so have I been forced to fly from my house, alone and friendless. I came to Pylos, thinking that so far from Argos, I might be safe from them, yet I found that even to Pylos did they follow me. But once I have left the mainland, I hope that they will weary of their search, and return to their lands in Argos.'

'I shall be glad indeed if I can help you,' said Telemachus, 'but the hospitality which I and my mother can offer you is not such as you would have received at my father's hands were he in his own house.' And as they sailed northwards, past the green fields of Elis, Telemachus told Theoclymenus about the suitors and the sorrow in his home. And all the time he was wondering whether he would reach that home alive, or whether the wooers would kill him, as they hoped.

But with Athene's help they sailed safely past the suitors' ambush, without a sight of Antinous' ship, steering clear of the little island midway in the strait, as she had bidden, and at dawn they reached the coast of Ithaca at a point distant from the town.

'Put me on shore here,' said Telemachus to Peiraeus, 'and go on with the ship to the harbour. There return her to good Noemon who lent her to me, then do you yourself guard the gifts that I have brought with me, until such time as I can take them to my house.'

'And what of me, my friend?' asked Theoclymenus. 'Shall I go to your house and there await you?'

Telemachus thought a moment. 'No,' he said, 'it were perhaps best that you did not go to my home until I am there myself.' Then turning to Peiraeus, he said, 'One more charge would I lay upon you, that you receive this stranger in your house until I return to the town and can myself be his host.'

Peiraeus smiled. 'Willingly,' he replied, 'shall I do as you ask, Telemachus. The stranger shall come with me.' And to Theoclymenus he said, 'You will be welcome among my family to such entertainment as we can offer, until the time when our prince can receive you in his own home.'

'I thank you all, you young men of Ithaca,' said Theoclymenus, 'I thank you with deep gratitude for your kindness and your hospitality.'

'The gods be with you all, stranger and friends, until I see you once again,' said Telemachus. And with that he set off to walk across the hills to the farm of Eumaeus, Odysseus' swineherd, where he lived with his grunting droves.

PART THREE

Odysseus in Ithaca

XIV

Eumaeus the Swineherd

MEANWHILE, on the shore of Ithaca, where the Phaeacian sailors had left him sleeping, Odysseus awoke, sat up and looked around. A light sea mist covered the rocky hills behind him and the water before him, obscuring all horizons, landward and seaward, and making unfamiliar all the country round about; so that Odysseus did not recognize his home.

He jumped to his feet. 'Truly I am an unhappy man,' he said to himself. 'I thought that I should have had my fill of dangers and of wandering, and yet here am I, cast away upon an unknown shore. Who would have believed those kindly seeming Phaeacians to be so base? Fool that I was to trust them and fall asleep upon their ship.'

But looking round him, Odysseus espied the gifts his

hosts had given him, all laid carefully upon the sand. He puzzled over them. 'If they had meant to steal my gifts they would not have left them here with me, yet if it was not shameful theft they had in mind, wherefore would they have deserted me in this strange land?' And with care he counted over the number of the gifts to see if there were any missing. For nigh on an hour he pondered, looking closely at each costly treasure, uncording the chests to count each cup and bowl or woven tunic that lay inside. But at length he found that as he remembered them to be, they were all there, and not a single gift was missing.

He was marvelling at this when he heard a merry whistling, and looked up to see a youth approaching him. The youth appeared from his garments to be a shepherd, but in reality it was Athene come to see how Odysseus had fared.

Odysseus was glad at the sight and called to her, 'Good shepherd, tell me, I pray you, what is this country? You are the first man I have seen upon it, and I trust that all your fellow countrymen are of as kindly an aspect as you, for I am utterly alone and friendless, and cast adrift in a strange land. Tell me, I beg of you, in what part of the world I may be.'

Athene answered him, 'In truth, stranger, this island may be small, but it is not mean nor barren, for all its size. Though it breeds no horses and has but little pasture-land, yet that pasture-land is rich, and the corn it grows in its little fields is among the finest man can find no matter where he seeks, and the wine pressed from the grapes that grow here is very sweet, and brings great joy to the drinker. Yes, stranger, I think that I speak truly when I say that even

K-M

in far-off unhappy Troy the name of Ithaca was not unknown.'

Odysseus was gladdened by her words, but as she was strange to him, and yet unproved, he would not let himself believe her and take her saying for truth; lest it might be once more his lot to be still far from his home, deceived and mocked at by a heartless stranger. So he hid his joy and hope and said, 'I have heard of Ithaca. In Crete, where I come from, men sometimes talked of Ithaca. I remember, now that I hear you speak the name. I have but even now sailed from my home in Crete, where I had the misfortune to kill a man who would have stolen from me these treasures you see here. When I found that he was dead I fled by night upon a ship with my possessions, meaning to go to Pylos, but the sailors cast me ashore while I was sleeping, together with all my goods.'

And Athene smiled at him and laughed a little, and changed her shape and became a lovely woman, tall and proud, in a glittering robe. 'You are ever my cunning Odysseus, my favourite among mortal men,' she said. 'Will you not leave your crafty ways even in your own Ithaca? I, among all the immortals, save only Father Zeus, am pre-eminent in wisdom and subtlety, as you among the mortals have no peer in craft and guile.' She smiled again. 'And yet you did not know me, Odysseus; I, Athene, who have been with you and guarded you through all your life. But for me you would not have reached your home, so angered with you was mighty Poseidon, lord of all the seas.'

'Great goddess,' said Odysseus, 'it is hard for a poor mortal to know you in the many guises that you take, but I thank you for all your years of aid. And now, I beseech you, deceive me not, but tell me truly, if this is really Ithaca. For with this mist that clouds the land, I cannot guess where I may be.'

Well pleased, Athene answered, 'Not even an immortal goddess is safe from the suspicions of your cautious mind, it seems. Yet that is why through all the years I have not deserted you. For you are such a man as I ever cherish, prudent, resourceful, and slow to be deceived. Yes, Odysseus, my friend, this is indeed Ithaca your home, and over the hills in your house, Penelope, your queen, awaits you. Look around you now, and see if you do not know your own dear island.'

And while she spoke the mist lifted from the hills and the sea, and as it rose, so were the last doubts and fears lifted from Odysseus' heart. He saw at once the old haunts that he knew so well, the places he had dreamed of with yearning for twenty years. He was standing on the beach of the little harbour of Phorcys, that was crowned by a great old olive-tree, near by the cavern that was called the Cave of the Naiads. And behind him, rising nobly over all, wrapped in a cloak of tall trees, stood Mount Neriton.

Odysseus knelt down and touched the sand and let it trickle through his fingers. He smiled up at Athene. 'It is indeed Ithaca,' he said, 'and I thank you for bringing me home at last.'

'You are home, my friend,' said Athene, 'but your troubles are not all ended. Come, let us first hide away the gifts the Phaeacians gave you, and then will I tell you what has come to pass in Ithaca while you have been away, and advise you what next to do.'

So Odysseus hid his treasures in the Cave of the Naiads,

until such time as he could fetch them to his house, and Athene set a great stone before the entrance to keep them safe. Then they sat down together, immortal goddess and mortal man, beneath the shade of the grey leaves of the huge olive-tree at the head of the harbour.

There Athene told Odysseus of the wooers, and the ruin they were causing in his house; and of how his faithful, loving wife, still hoping in her heart for his return, kept them waiting for an answer, day after day; and of how the wicked men were plotting to kill his son as he sailed home from Pylos.

'It is well for me,' said Odysseus when she had done, 'that I have you to protect me, else should I have gone at once to my home, perhaps only to be slain in my own hall by these villains. But tell me, goddess, what it were best that I should do, and be with me still. For if I knew that there were three hundred of these men, I would fight against them all and rout them, if you were by my side, inspiring me with your divine courage, as you ever did in the old days at Troy.'

'I have no doubt that you would, my brave Odysseus. You need have no fear, for I shall not desert you now. But let us not go openly into this matter, let us enter it with craft and subtlety, in a way such as you and I delight in. First shall I make you old and like a beggar, so that you may be unknown to those who might recognize you, and of no account in the sight of all, even in the eyes of your own wife and son. Then must you go to the farm of Eumaeus your swineherd, who has been your devoted servant all these years. Tell him not who you are, but ask him concerning all that has befallen in your house, and from him will you learn much. Meanwhile, I shall go to Sparta and warn Telemachus, who is even now in the palace of mighty Menelaus, of how the suitors seek to kill him as he returns from Pylos.'

'Let it be as you say, great goddess,' replied Odysseus, 'it is a scheme such as I ever love. But I would ask you one thing first. Why is it that you, to whom all things are possible, should have sent Telemachus upon this vain journey to Pylos and to Sparta, endangering his life at the hands of these men? Surely you could not wish that he too should face perils such as I have met with in my travels?'

'Do not be disturbed on his account, Odysseus, for I shall guard him well, and, indeed, at this very moment he sits feasting in the house of Menelaus, rejoicing in the kindness of his host and fair Queen Helen. I did but send him forth on this quest for tidings of your homecoming—though well I knew he would find none—that he might prove his manhood and live through an adventure, however small compared with yours, that would show him to be a son worthy of his father. And now I must away to Sparta.'

Athene rose and touched Odysseus on the brow, and instantly he grew aged, becoming, in as many seconds, thirty years older. The skin of his face shrivelled into wrinkles and his hair became sparse and grey, his arms and legs lost their firmness and his sharp blue eyes grew dim. Clothed in a ragged tunic through which his spare ribs showed, and an ancient leather jerkin, with a battered wallet such as travellers carry, and a staff in his hand, he was even such a beggar as might be seen, any day, crouching at the gate of a rich man's house, whining for alms.

'No one in Ithaca will recognize you now,' she said.

'Nobody will guess you to be Odysseus the king. Go to the swineherd's house and wait, and there will I come to you again. Until that time, farewell.' And instantly she vanished from his sight as though she had never been with him, for such are the ways of the immortal gods.

Odysseus at once set off along the track from the beach that would lead him through a nearby wood and over the hills to the swineherd's farm. In the wood the path was cool and shaded, and the birds sang in the trees; but as it wound up the hillside it was bare and rugged, and the sun shone down fiercely upon the grey rocks and the clumps of scented thyme. And every step of the way was familiar to Odysseus, and it seemed to him as though he could remember each tree and crag, and he rejoiced as he walked once more in his own Ithaca.

Eumaeus, the faithful swineherd, had built the farm to keep his master's swine after Odysseus had sailed for Troy, so to Odysseus the house itself was unknown. It was a small house of wood and stone, with a sheltering porch and a roof of logs overlaid with clay, and it stood in a wide yard surrounded by a strong wall of stones and a thick thorn hedge. In the yard, around the walls, were twelve large sties, and in each of them were fifty sows and their little grunting piglets.

Three of the four men who helped Eumaeus herd the swine had taken them to the edge of the wood to feed on roots and acorns, while the fourth had driven a fat pig into the town, that the suitors might have pork for their feasting. So when Odysseus approached the farm, Eumaeus was alone, sitting on a bench before his porch, fashioning himself a pair of sandals from a strong piece of leather.

Odysseus pushed open the gate and entered the courtyard, and immediately the four savage hounds which the swineherd kept as watchdogs rushed upon him, barking and growling; and he would most assuredly have been hurt had he not had the good sense to remain quite still and incite them no further. Eumaeus heard the barking, and dropping his sandals on the ground, he ran to the gate, calling off the dogs.

Odysseus laughed. 'It is plain to see,' he said, 'that your dogs do not like strangers. But you must find in them a most sure protection for your swine.'

'It was well for you, old man,' said Eumaeus with agitation, 'that you did not attempt to run away, for if you had, the dogs would surely have thought you were a thief and torn you in pieces. And I have troubles enough on my shoulders, with my good master wandering the gods alone know where, and his house full of shameless gluttons, without a man being killed upon my doorstep by my own dogs. But come, old stranger, you are very welcome to my house, though the dogs may have made you doubt it. Come in with me and rest and eat, and we will talk together.'

Odysseus thanked him and followed him into the little house, and there Eumaeus bade the master whom he had not recognized, so well had Athene altered his appearance, sit down upon a couch of reeds and brushwood covered with a goat-skin, which served him for a bed, while he threw more sticks upon the fire burning on the hearth. Odysseus was well pleased with this kindly welcome, and sitting down and holding out his hands to the blaze, he said, 'May fate reward you, good swineherd, for your friendliness, and give you your heart's desire.'

'My heart's desire?' repeated Eumaeus. 'It is not likely I shall gain that.' He fetched his strip of leather from the porch and began to roll it up. 'I had a good master once,' he said. 'He was just and generous and kindly, and what more in a master could any slave want? But he went away to fight in a far-off land, and after twenty years he has still not yet come home. I have no doubt but that he has perished, struck down by the sword of a foe, or wrecked upon the ocean, and I shall never see him more. In the years of his absence have I served him faithfully, and his herds of swine have prospered and increased in numbers, in spite of the many slaughtered wastefully of late. Were my master but here to know it, he would reward me, I am certain. But he never comes, though I wait and hope. So there is nothing left for me but to live on, serving faithfully the memory of a good and kindly lord. But you will be hungry, old stranger, and I doubt not but that you have troubles of your own, so let us eat and drink, for good food and wine bring a measure of contentment to those who have a share of them.'

Eumaeus roasted a joint of pork over the fire and mixed sweet wine and water in a wooden bowl; and when the meal was ready he sat down beside Odysseus. 'This food, though good enough, is not such as is eaten in my master's house,' he said. 'The best and fattest of the swine are taken by the suitors of my master's wife. They spend their days and half their nights lording it in his house, guzzling his food and drinking all his wine. My master's son is very young yet, and my master's wife is but a woman, and there is no man to forbid these wooers. My lord was a rich man, with many flocks and herds and much fertile land, more than any twenty other men on this island might possess together. But even his riches are not measureless and his beasts are not without number, and the grain from his cornfields and the wine from his grapes will not endure for ever, if the waste of food and drink continues, that goes on daily in his house at the command of these insolent suitors.'

'Tell me, my friend, the name of this master of yours, for it may be that in my travels I have met with news of him.'

'Old man,' replied Eumaeus, 'every beggar and every wanderer that comes to Ithaca and would have hospitality, goes to my master's wife and to his young son with a tale of having met my lord, or having heard of his whereabouts, or having seen him once, or what you will. And most of the tales are lies, but they serve to earn the teller a good supper. No, Queen Penelope and young Telemachus have long since ceased to believe these stories. They are only distressed by them and grieve yet more for their lost king. For you must know that my lord was king of all Ithaca, noble Odysseus, Laertes' son. Even now I speak his name with reverence, for his care for me was great, and he is still my master, though I may never see him again.'

Odysseus drank his wine slowly. 'Odysseus, king of Ithaca,' he said. 'I know the name well, and I can promise you, one day and not so far distant, he will return to his home and take vengeance on all those who have treated with insolence his wife and his son, and wasted his wealth.'

'I do indeed wish that I could find it in my heart to believe you, old stranger. For I desire nothing more than that King Odysseus should return to his home, and that soon. But it must be that he has perished in the wars, or been drowned with all his men, for in twenty years we have heard no word of him. Yet do I grieve for him ceaselessly, and long for a homecoming that I dare not expect. And for his son Telemachus, a princely youth and handsome, do I also grieve, for he has sailed but lately to Pylos to seek tidings of his father, and I have heard a rumour that those wicked suitors have sent a ship to lie in wait for him on his return and kill him. If it be true or false I know not, though it is most likely true, for I would put no evil past them, even to the slaying of their host. May all the gods protect him, for there is naught that I and those who love him can do for him. But come, old stranger, tell me of yourself awhile, and let me think on other things than the sorrows of Odysseus' house.'

So they talked together until the sun went down the sky, and many were the entertaining and lying tales Odysseus told the swineherd about himself; both to give the good man amusement and to cheer him, and to make quite certain that he himself was not recognized.

Close on sunset Eumaeus prepared the supper for his four men and his guest; and just as the sun was sinking behind the hills, with a great squealing and grunting, those swine who slept within the pens were driven into the yard by the men and securely enclosed.

The six of them sat down to supper, and after they had eaten and drunk they stayed beside the fire and talked. While they talked the night wind rose and blew howling from the hills; a wet west wind, sending the clouds across the moon and the rain beating on the house walls.

'It will be a wet and chilly night,' said Eumaeus.

Odysseus reflected that in his beggar's guise he had no

warm cloak to wrap himself in when he lay down to sleep; and as a jest for his own diversion, he decided to test his swineherd's hospitality, and see whether or not he would offer a poor wanderer the comforts of a cloak for the night. He drank off the last of the wine from his wooden cup and smiled. 'My friends,' he said, 'I am not so young as all of you, and my head is not so strong. I fear that your good wine has confused my wits a little. But what matter if I am a little drunk? It shall make me bold to tell you a tale of the time when I fought at Troy. In those days I was no beggarman, wandering from town to town, suing for my bread from those more fortunate than I. No, I was a warrior of no mean might, and oft I fought alongside the great Odysseus himself. One evening we lay in ambush under the walls of the city. Odysseus and Menelaus, king of Sparta, were our leaders, and I was the third in command. We crouched below the walls in the dusk, all among the coarse reeds on the boggy ground, and while we waited, night came on, even such a night as this, cold and wet and windy, with sleet and the cold north wind. Alone of all the others I was without my cloak, for when we had set forth from the camp the evening had been mild. Now while the others lay and dozed, wrapped warmly in their cloaks, I shivered in my tunic and cursed my folly. At length I could bear the cold no longer, and leaning across to Odysseus, who was beside me, I shook his shoulder, whispering, "Odysseus, I shall be dead by morning, I am so cold. You wily one, tell me if there is aught that I can do to save my life."

'Odysseus whispered back to me, "Be silent now, for I have a plan that will win a cloak for you, but it must not be suspected by the others." With that he raised himself upon his elbow and spoke to our comrades. "My friends," he said, "I have just had a dream, it must surely have come from the immortal gods, in which it seemed to me that it would be a wise thing if one of us were to return to the ships and ask Agamemnon, our leader, if he will send us more men for the ambush, for we are but a small party and far from the camp."

'No sooner had he spoken than a young man rose, flung off his cloak, and ran swiftly back towards the shore.

' "There is your cloak," Odysseus whispered to me, "just as I promised you."

'And in it I slept comfortably until the dawn.' Odysseus paused, and Eumaeus and the others laughed.

'That is a good tale, stranger,' said the swineherd, 'and I see well the point of it. We are all poor here and have but one cloak apiece, yet is there one to spare which we keep aside lest in stormy weather one of us should be drenched to the skin in the rain. That shall you have tonight, and if our good Prince Telemachus should come safely home from Pylos, I can promise you that he will give you a warm cloak for yourself and a new tunic without rags and patches, for he is ever generous, as was his father.'

Eumaeus made a bed of reeds beside the fire and spread upon it rugs of sheepskin, and when Odysseus had laid himself down, he covered him with the spare cloak and wished him a good night.

The other men lay down upon their beds of brushwood, but Eumaeus cared not to leave the swine unguarded when the night was wild, so flinging around him his thick mantle, and taking up a spear, he went out from the house to where the boars were sleeping, beyond the courtyard gate, beneath a high rock which sheltered them from the wind and the rain, and there he spent the night. And Odysseus was glad to see the care his honest herdsman took of his master's swine.

XV

Odysseus meets his Son

TOWARDS morning the wind dropped, and the driven rain ceased, and for a short space the stars shone in the blue night-sky. But soon they faded at the approach of dawn and the green and saffron streaks of light low down in the east changed to pink and gold and spread across the sky; while the sun rose up above the sea, like a fiery ball coming from the water to proclaim the start of a fair, calm day.

At the first light of dawn Eumaeus returned to his house, and very early the four swineherds set out with the pigs, driving them forth from the yard grunting eagerly, and they themselves, wrapped in their cloaks, for the morning was still fresh, were carrying each a wallet filled with bread and meat, and a flask of wine.

Odysseus and Eumaeus were left alone, and Eumaeus set to work to prepare breakfast for himself and his guest. He raked away the ashes and blew upon the embers and flung sticks upon the smouldering wood, and soon there was a fine fire blazing. Then making a paste of barley flour and water with a little honey, he kneaded it into cakes and set them upon a hot stone in the midst of the fire.

After they had enjoyed their meal, Eumaeus fed the sows in their sties and busied himself about the tasks of the farm, while Odysseus helped him, fetching water and collecting faggots and sweeping the yard.

During the day they talked together, and Odysseus said, 'It is not right that I should longer be a burden to you. Tomorrow I shall walk down to the town and see if begging will gain me meals in the houses of the noblemen of Ithaca, for I must not stay here, eating the food and drinking the wine you and your men can so ill spare. Let the rich show their generosity for a change. Besides, I have a mind to go to the house of my old comrade Odysseus and see for myself how things stand there. Maybe the suitors will be glad to grant to an unfortunate wanderer some scraps of another man's food. Yet I would not expect their charity for nothing, and I shall be ready to do services for them, running errands, chopping wood, and waiting on them at table.'

But Eumaeus would not hear of it. 'So long as I have any food and drink to offer you,' he said, 'you shall not need to beg. My friend, you are welcome to stay up here in the farm as long as you please. And do not think that in the house of Odysseus you will get a welcome from the suitors of the queen. No, they would rather do you an injury, throwing you from the doors and cursing you, than give you a portion of the food they eat. And their servants are not staid, honest, aged men the like of yourself; they are sleek, insolent rogues, much resembling their masters in many ways. No, my old friend, wait up here with us, and when and if young Lord Telemachus comes home, he will give you food and clothing, I am sure of that.'

Later, Odysseus asked the swineherd for news of his parents, saying, 'In the days when I knew him, Odysseus often spoke of noble Laertes and gentle Anticleia, his much-loved father and mother. Tell me, good swineherd, what has befallen them?'

'Laertes still lives, though Lady Anticleia is dead, worn out by sorrowing for her lost son. Truly, it is a sad death to die, to pine away before one's time through grief for a beloved child. Lord Laertes, saddened by her loss and ever grieving for my master, and unable to bear longer the insolence of the suitors, left the house and went to live upon his farm across the hills from the town. There he passes his days in toiling in the fields, labouring in a way most unfitting for the father of a king. Though indeed, no one could wonder that he cares not to live in my master's house, watching the wooers despoiling the estate and making merry in the home of his absent son. I myself go seldom to the house these days, preferring to send one of my men with the fatted hogs for the feasting, for I grow angry to look upon such waste. Though in the old days, while yet Lady Anticleia lived, I went often to wait on her, for she had been good and kind to me from the time I was a little child, caring for me as though I had been one of her own children, rather than a slave.'

The remembrance of his mother, whose spirit he had met in Hades' land, filled Odysseus' heart with sorrow; and to forget his woes and to hide his grief from Eumaeus, he said quickly, 'Yesterday I told you many tales of my life and misfortunes, do you now tell me of your own birth and parentage, and of how you became a slave, for I am sure that so goodly a man as you is no mean peasant, but rather the son of some free and noble lord.'

'You are right, old friend,' replied the swineherd, 'I was not born in slavery, and my father was a king. The story of my early years makes an unhappy tale, yet, because you ask, will I tell it to you. There is an island called Syrie, you may have heard of it. Few people dwell there, for all that it is rich in pasture-land where graze fine flocks and herds. And the cornfields on Syrie are like a golden sea at harvest time, and the vineyards bear fine purple grapes, so that never there comes famine or pestilence or poverty, but all the people live secure and safe, dying peacefully of old age. There are two cities on Syrie, and my father was king over them both, ruling well and wisely. To the island, once or twice a year, came the Phoenicians from the city of Sidon, with merchandise to sell; necklaces, bracelets, little jars of perfume, and great bales of cloth all piled up in their ship. Tall, handsome rogues they were, with striped head-dresses and golden rings, well able to drive a bargain by their wheedling ways, and with ever a lie on their lips. In my father's house there was a Phoenician woman, bought many years before from pirates. Comely she was, and skilled in all women's crafts, and often would I play by her side while she went about her work. One day as she was washing garments in the river close by its mouth, where it flowed into the sea, the traders from her country put in to the shore. One of them talked with her, asking her whence she came, for he guessed from her looks and stature that she was a woman of Phoenicia.

'"I am from Sidon," she replied, "and my father is a rich man there. But I was stolen from my home by pirates and sold to the king of this little island."

'And the man said to her, "If you would see your home once more, have patience until the day our trading here is finished and we set sail for Sidon, and we will take you back with us and see you safely to your father's house."

'To this the woman agreed gladly, bidding the merchant tell no one on Syrie of his promise. "If you should see me in my master's house, when you bring your wares there to sell, or if you should pass me in the street at any time, make as though we have never spoken together before, for I would not have anyone suspect what we have in mind." She told him further, "My master here is rich, and when your trading is done and you send me word that I am to come to you, I will bring with me much gold and silver from his store-room. Nay, more than that, he has a little son who loves me well and ever joys to be by my side, him will I bring with me, for he should fetch a good price in Sidon, more than gold and silver. And what others could do when they sold me to my master, the same can I do to his child."

'For some months, as was their wont, the Phoenicians remained on Syrie, selling and bartering and making great profit. When at length the time came for them to depart, one of their number came to my father's house with a necklace of amber beads linked with gold. Such a pretty thing it was that all my mother's women crowded round to see it while she held it in her hands, wondering whether the price was too high. But unseen by the others, the merchant signed to the Phoenician woman, and she nodded back in token that she had understood. When he had left the house with the price of the necklace in the leathern pursc at his belt, she took my hand and bade me come with her to walk upon the shore. As we passed through the great hall of my father's house, she picked up three golden goblets from a table and hid them in her cloak. I asked her what she did, but she only told me to be silent and hurried me through the doors. We went past the city and down to the harbour where waited the Phoenician ship. She took me on board and the merchants set sail, and I never saw my home again. Many days later the ship touched at Ithaca, and the men went to the town to trade, taking me with them. They sold me for a slave to Lord Laertes, in whose house I found only kindness, and good Lady Anticleia cared well for me. So in the end, my misfortunes were not as heavy as they might have been.'

'Truly, Eumaeus, your fate could have been much harder, as you say,' said Odysseus. 'Indeed, your sorrows are no worse than mine, who am a wanderer and a beggar.'

Since he had found that the swineherd would not let him go to town, Odysseus was easily able to remain at the farm awaiting Athene's commands, and he passed the next day in a similar fashion to the first, helping Eumaeus and talking much.

It was at dawn on the following day that Telemachus reached Ithaca in safety, and in obedience to Athene's words, sent Noemon's ship on to the harbour and set out alone to walk to the swineherd's house.

As on the two previous mornings, when the other men had gone forth with the swine, Eumaeus made ready to cook the breakfast. Odysseus was sitting on a stool facing the open door, and through it he saw someone entering the yard. Immediately the dogs rushed forward, but in greeting, joyously wagging their tails, barking and leaping up at the newcomer; yet in quite a different fashion from the way in which they had barked and leapt at Odysseus, two days before.

Odysseus, who guessed at once who the young man must be who patted the shaggy heads of the dogs and called to them by name, said to Eumaeus, 'There is a friend of yours on his way to your house, someone whom your dogs know and like, for they are giving him a welcome quite unlike the one they gave me when I came here the other day.'

He had hardly spoken before Telemachus stood in the doorway, and the swineherd jumped up with a cry of joy, dropping from his hands the wooden bowl in which he had been mixing the wine, so that it was all spilt upon the floor.

'My dear young master,' he exclaimed, 'you have come safely home! Indeed, I feared that I should never see you more when I heard rumours of the suitors' plot. It is a happiness that I had not dared to hope for, to greet you once more in Ithaca. But come inside, my dear prince, and sit down, that I may enjoy your company, for it is not often in these days that you find time to come to the farm.'

Telemachus embraced the swineherd with affection. 'I am trusting, my dear good friend,' he said, 'that you will give me word of all that has befallen in my father's house since the day I sailed for Pylos. How fares my mother? Is she still steadfast in her sorrowing for my father, or has she at last made up her mind to take another husband?'

'If she had made her choice from among the suitors, news of it would have been brought to me even here. No, dear prince, she still waits and hopes with patience.'

As Telemachus entered the house, Odysseus rose and offered him his place, as was a fitting gesture from a beggar to a prince.

But Telemachus said with courtesy, 'Do not disturb yourself, stranger, I beg of you, let me find myself somewhere else to sit. It is not seemly that a younger man should take an elder's place.'

Odysseus was pleased to see that his son showed respect even to a ragged wanderer and displayed no arrogance, though he was the son of a king.

Eumaeus laid a sheepskin upon a pile of brushwood beside the fire for Telemachus. 'This stranger and I were about to breakfast,' he said, 'will you not share our meal with us?' And he set cold meat in wooden platters beside the three of them, and laid a basket of bread on the floor between his guests, and bade them eat, while he mixed more wine and water to replace that which he had spilt.

When the meal was over, with a kindly smile at Odysseus, Telemachus asked, 'Tell me, Eumaeus, whence comes the stranger? And is there aught that I can do for him?'

'He has told me the story of all his woes and wanderings,' replied Eumaeus, 'and a grievous tale it is. But now he is come to Ithaca, for once he knew King Odysseus in the days when they both fought at Troy, and would seek what help he can in the house of his old war-time comrade.'

Telemachus frowned a little in embarrassment. 'Stranger, I would gladly welcome you to my father's house, and so too would my good mother. But I have no authority in my own home, and she is but a woman. For in the house of Odysseus his wife's suitors order all things as they will, and I fear that if you come down to us they will offer you some insult ill fitted to your years when I am not by; or indeed, it may be in my very presence, for they care not for me either, counting me but a child. And they may well be dangerous now and seek to do me and my friends some hurt, since I escaped unharmed from their ambush in the strait.'

'It is surely pitiful when a man is thus oppressed in his own home,' said Odysseus. 'Would that your father might return and scatter all these evil men.'

'I thank you for that wish, good stranger, and echo it with all my heart. But see that you remain here in safety with Eumaeus for so long as it shall please you, and I will send you food and wine in plenty, and new clothes.' He turned to the swineherd. 'And now, Eumaeus, my good friend, I have a task for you. Will you go down to the town and bear word of my safe return to my mother? For I would not have her left longer in torturing doubt. Yet see that you tell no one else but her, for the sooner her wooers learn of my escape, the sooner they will think out another base deed against me. Meanwhile,' he smiled, 'if you can bear with another guest, I will stay on the farm with you for a day or two, while I think out what it is best for me to do.'

'Gladly will I have you here with me, dear prince,' said Eumaeus, 'for then I know at least that you are safe, when I have you before my eyes. And I will go at once and tell the queen, and her alone, that you are back in Ithaca. But should I not also go to Lord Laertes on his farm and tell him the welcome news? For I doubt not but that he too has heard the rumour of the suitors' plot and will be grieving for his grandson's plight.'

Telemachus thought a moment, then he replied, 'No, it is best that you come back here quickly with tidings of how things fare at home. Ask my mother to send a servant she can trust, good Eurycleia perhaps, with word of my return to my grandfather, that he may no longer grieve for me.'

So Eumaeus went to bear to Penelope the tidings of Telemachus' return, and Odysseus was left alone with his son. But before either of them had time to speak, Odysseus, from his seat opposite the door, saw Athene, once again in the likeness of a lovely woman in a shining robe, standing on the threshold. Telemachus saw her not, only Odysseus and the dogs were aware that she stood there. And the four hounds, recognizing her for a more than mortal being, neither barked nor growled, but slunk away with their tails between their legs, and crouched down by the house wall, whimpering. Telemachus heard their whining and turned to look out into the yard, but though he looked straight at Athene, he could not see her, for it was only to Odysseus that she had chosen to appear. She beckoned to him and he rose and went outside and followed her out of the sight of his son.

'The time has come, Odysseus,' said Athene, 'for you to

disclose yourself to your son, that together you may plot the destruction of the suitors. Make your plans and go to the town with speed, for I am eager to see those shameless men reap their just reward. And remember, my friend, I shall be with you, even though you may not see me there.'

And she touched Odysseus, and once more he became his true self, a strong straight man of two score years and a little over. Again his dark hair hung in curls about his shoulders and his eyes were bright and keen. Even his very clothes were no longer the garments of an old beggarman, for he wore a rich tunic of snowy white, and a short fringed mantle of blue. And immediately upon the change, Athene vanished.

Odysseus returned to the house, and when Telemachus saw how he had been transformed, he was afraid. He started to his feet, and in spite of himself he backed towards the wall. 'Stranger,' he said fearfully, 'you are not as you were but a few moments past. Indeed, you must be one of the immortal gods. I pray you, be compassionate to me and to my house, and I and my mother will offer you much sacrifice.'

Odysseus smiled. 'Have no fear, Telemachus, I am not a god. I am your own father, Odysseus, come home at last.' And he made as though to embrace his son.

But Telemachus had inherited a measure of his father's caution, and he would not believe him. 'No,' he said, 'you are rather one of the immortals come to deceive me so that I may have still more sorrow. For but now you were ragged and old and like a beggar, and yet in so short a space of time you have become like a mighty king. Only an immortal could accomplish that. I implore you, do me no harm, for I have suffered much already.'

'My son,' replied Odysseus, 'why will you not believe that it is really I, your father? It has been with the aid of all-wise Athene that I have reached Ithaca after years of wandering. And she it is who made me to resemble the old beggar whom you saw until now, so that no one might recognize me as Odysseus. And though you saw her not, she appeared to me but a moment ago, and gave me back my own shape that you and I might know each other. Wondrous it is that such things can be, but to the immortal gods they are easy.'

Telemachus looked well at him and believed his words, and suddenly realizing that Odysseus had come home and all his hopes for that safe return were fulfilled and all his fears were ended, he flung himself in his father's arms and wept in sweet relief.

'How did you reach Ithaca, father? In what ship? Tell me everything.'

'The kindly men of Phaeacia brought me home and left me safely on the beach in the harbour of Phorcys with all the gifts that they had given me. The gifts have I stowed in the Cave of the Naiads until such time as we can fetch them. But all my adventures will I relate to you presently, for now we must decide together how best to destroy the suitors. Tell me how many there are, and whether they are warriors or weaklings, so that I may know if we two alone should have any chance against them.'

'Dear father,' protested Telemachus, 'I have heard from all who knew you that you were ever a mighty fighter, but this task that you would try is too hard even for you.

Two men alone could not fight against the suitors. Why, there are above a hundred of them altogether, and we should soon be slain. Twelve young noblemen there are from Ithaca, and the rest from the islands close by. Two and fifty from Dulichium with their six serving-men, four and twenty from Same, and from Zacynthus, twenty. No, father, we two should have no chance against so many.'

'Athene herself has promised me her help, my son. What say you to Athene as a comrade-in-arms?'

'If she will aid us,' said Telemachus thoughtfully, 'our cause may prosper, though we shall have a bitter fight.'

'Let us believe we shall gain a great victory,' said Odysseus, 'and lay our plans with confidence. Best would it be if you were to return home at dawn tomorrow. Go among the suitors as though you did not suspect them of having tried to kill you, be affable and friendly towards them. And I, in the likeness of a beggar, as I was before, will come to the house with Eumaeus. There shall I act as though I had come for alms, meantime watching carefully the wooers, that I may make my further plans. If what you and the swineherd say of them is true, then will they most likely insult me and mistreat me. But do not forget, to all others I am an old beggarman and not your father, and suffer these insolent men to treat me as they will, for we shall, in the end, take vengeance on them. For above all, no one else but you must know that I have come home, not even your mother.'

And so they talked together and laid their plans; but in the evening, Odysseus looked up and saw Athene at the door. She touched him and smiled and vanished, and once again he became old and ragged, so that he knew Eumaeus must be on his way home. And indeed, in a few moments the good swineherd appeared, and they greeted him eagerly and asked him his news.

'What tidings have you for us of the happenings in your master's house?' inquired Odysseus.

'And what of my mother, was she glad to hear that I am safe?' asked Telemachus.

'Indeed, my prince, she rejoiced much at the news.'

'And the suitors who sailed to kill me, have they returned yet to the town?'

'I did not stay long enough to discover that,' replied Eumaeus, 'I thought it better to return home at once. Yet it can make but little difference, for as I was going to the apartments of the queen with my message, a young man, who, it seems, had sailed with you, came also to the house to tell her you were back in Ithaca. But not content with telling her, he shouted out his tidings to all around as he went through the hall. Therefore the suitors are aware already that their plot has failed.'

Telemachus sighed, and then he brightened, remembering how his father had come home. 'We have had labours enough for one day,' he said, 'let us eat and drink and take our rest. Come, Eumaeus, and you, good stranger.' And Telemachus smiled at his father when the swineherd was not looking and Odysseus smiled back at him, in the way two people smile at one another when they share a secret, known only to the two of them.

XVI

Penelope and her Suitors

WHEN the suitors heard that Telemachus had returned unharmed to Ithaca, they grew angry and dejected; for they thought that not again might they have such an opportunity to kill him, secretly and far from his home, and in such a way that they themselves should not be blamed for his death.

'It is a great misfortune for us, that our plans have come to naught,' said Eurymachus. 'But let us at once send forth a ship to tell Antinous and our other friends that Telemachus has slipped through the ambush. Otherwise will they wait on for him in the strait between Ithaca and Same, wasting their time without profit.'

They set off for the town to find a ship, but on the way, one of them, pointing out to sea, said, 'Surely that is the ship good Antinous sailed off in, making her way to the coast? He must have seen Telemachus escape him, and is coming home.'

They went down to the harbour to meet Antinous and his twenty comrades; and when the ship was moored they all went together to the assembly place. They turned away a few men who had gathered there to pass the time in idle talk, saying that they had private matters to discuss; and posted two of their number to keep a watch on any of the other townsfolk who should come that way, lest they should overhear them.

Antinous spoke first with harsh anger in his voice. 'Day and night we kept watch for Telemachus,' he said, 'but yet we missed him. One of the gods must have helped him, or he never could have escaped our net. But though he has evaded us this time, let us not waver in our design to kill him, for until he is removed we shall not prosper in Odysseus' house, and the queen's determination to give us no answer and make no choice of a husband will be, as now, strengthened by his support. Do you not all agree with me?'

He paused, and there were murmurs of assent; but a few of the wooers objected, saying, 'We are playing a dangerous game, Antinous. Easy is it to say, "Let us kill him," but he is a man and the son of a king, and not an outcast or a wild animal to be hunted and slain for sport. And things will go ill with all of us if we are found to have murdered him.'

Several voices of those who had until then supported Antinous were raised in agreement, and Antinous frowned blackly, biting his lips. 'My friends,' he said, 'you are foolish. Have you not thought that Telemachus may know that we tried to take his life as he returned from Pylos? And if he knows, surely he will not rest until he has called together the men of Ithaca and denounced us to them? He will stir up the people against us, and those of you who come from the neighbouring islands will have to return home without a wife; while we who are townsmen of Ithaca will have to flee to another land until the trouble is forgotten. No, my friends, Telemachus must die, it is the only way for us to secure not only success in our wooing of the queen, but our own safety.'

They were afraid when they heard his words, for few of them had considered that Telemachus might tell the people of their treachery, for, in spite of the determination he had shown in his decision to sail for Pylos, they had grown into the way, through many years, of thinking him a child who put his faith in all others older than himself and was content always to be bidden what to do. 'You are right, Antinous,' they said, 'Telemachus must die, and that before he has time to call an assembly.'

Antinous smiled in satisfaction. 'We must fall upon him in some place far from the town,' he said. 'For suspicion must not come to rest on us, nor must we risk the townsfolk's witnessing his death. When he goes to overlook one of his farms, perhaps, or when he visits old Lord Laertes, we must lie in wait for him as he comes alone along the road, and slay him swiftly. We must watch for an opportunity and not let it slip, for as long as he remains in the house, he is safe. We cannot kill him there without the truth being known to every man. Are you all in agreement with me?'

Though most of the suitors spoke for him, there were still

a few who were silent, counting the plot too dangerous to themselves. These Antinous addressed, saying, 'There is no alternative to this, my friends, save only that we all depart for our own homes, abandoning our efforts to win the fair Penelope.'

'That we will never do,' they cried.

'Then must Telemachus die,' said Antinous.

'You are right,' they said. 'We are with you over this, good Antinous, every one of us.'

Antinous was pleased at the success of his persuasion. 'Let us all return now to Odysseus' house,' he said, 'and wait to see how Telemachus greets us when he comes. For from his manner we may haply guess if he intends to tell the people of our plot to kill him on his journey from Pylos, or indeed, whether he has learnt of it or not.'

Together they all walked back to the house and sat down in the great hall, talking and dicing and playing draughts, apparently with no other care in the world but to amuse themselves and pass away the time as pleasantly as possible. But the minds of many of them were filled with thoughts of ways and means of murder, and all of them were wondering if and when Telemachus would come back to the house.

By the time that the suitors had returned to her husband's house, Penelope's first joy and relief at the swineherd's news had grown calmer; and she, who all through the days of distraction and grief, while Telemachus was with Menelaus, had not dared to face them, now made up her mind to go down to the hall and confront the men who would have killed her son.

She called her maids and bade them bring out a splendid

robe, and they were glad and ran to do her bidding eagerly. For she had had no care for what she wore since Medon the herald had told her of the suitors' plot, but had sat, silent and disconsolate, her clothes awry and her hair dishevelled, speaking to no one, and ordering away with a gesture all who had tried to ask her what was amiss. So now they went willingly and fetched her three robes to choose from; two of them white with embroidered borders, and the other palest saffron yellow with a woven band of stiff, formal flowers in red, and a scarlet fringe. She chose the yellow robe and put it on, fastening it at each shoulder with a golden brooch which she took from a little silver casket. Her handmaidens then combed her hair into seven long curls, held in place by ribbons around her head; three tresses down her back, one upon each shoulder, and two on her breast. Then over all her head and round about her white throat she flung a crimson veil, so fine that through it her bright hair could be seen.

When all had been done, she told three of her maids to come with her, and descended the stairs from her apartments, passing through the women's quarters on her way to the hall. In the doorway she paused, looking in on the company of the wooers, and disdain and contempt for them filled her heart.

One of the suitors saw her and rose, crying out, 'It is the queen!' And instantly the eyes of all were turned towards the door at the far end of the hall which led to the other rooms of the house.

'Greetings, fair Queen Penelope,' they called to her. 'It is not often lately that you have honoured us with your presence.'

But her eyes searched the hall for Antinous, their acknowledged leader, and she looked hard at him. 'Have you no shame, Antinous,' she said with scorn, 'that you still dare to show your face in my husband's house after the evil you sought to do his son? I have heard it said of you that you are the flower of all the young men of Ithaca, wise in counsel and fair in speech.' She laughed bitterly. 'In the three long years and more that you have been daily in this house, my son and I have learnt to know differently. The flower of the young nobility of Ithaca! Thus may men be mistaken who only see you as you walk abroad in the pride of your wealth and birth. But I who have seen you throughout these years, eating another man's food and drinking his wine, all uninvited; I who have seen into the black caverns of your evil heart, cannot be deceived by any outward show.'

She paused, and Antinous and all the other suitors were silent, not knowing any reply to make her. Angrily she went on, her voice ringing through the hall, 'How could you try to kill Telemachus, Antinous? You out of all the others. Have you forgotten how, when you were yet a child, your father Eupeithes joined once with the Taphian pirates and went a-plundering? The anger of all the men of Ithaca was against him, and in his sore distress he fled for help to Odysseus his king. Yes, Antinous, he came to the father of Telemachus, and Odysseus defended him against the crowd, and with his wise and sober counsel won his people to hold their hands and seek no more to do violence to Eupeithes and his house.' Her voice grew softer, 'Oh, Antinous, have a thought for past favours, devour no more my husband's goods, have no evil intentions

against his son, and desist from your hated wooing of Odysseus' wife; and bid your fellow suitors do the like.'

For a time all were quiet in the hall, and they watched her without speaking any word, while they all debated in their minds what it were best to say. Antinous frowned at the table before him, and tossed angrily from one hand to another the dice he had been playing with when Penelope had entered; but he could think of nothing that he might say to her.

It was Eurymachus, who, recovering his composure first, answered her with his customary soft words. 'Gracious queen, and fairest of all the noble ladies on Ithaca and the neighbouring isles, be not distressed by all these things, for they are but the imaginations of your troubled mind, which, by too much grieving for your lord, has been made ready ever to accept fresh sorrows but never to admit more joyous happenings. Or perhaps they are but the rumours whispered in your ears by those, who, through their spite and jealousy, would discredit us with you. For we suitors of the loveliest lady in the land would never seek to harm her son, no more indeed than we would seek to injure her, and what than that could be farther from our thoughts?'

'Your tongue is glib, Eurymachus,' said Penelope, 'it was ever so.'

'No, dearest queen, you do me wrong. Indeed, you wrong us all, I beg you to believe me. We wish no evil to Telemachus, for is he not the beloved son of the woman we most wish to please?' He turned from one to another of his companions, 'My friends, tell me, is that not so?'

And with one accord they called out eagerly, 'It is the truth, Eurymachus.'

Eurymachus smiled at Penelope. 'You see, fair queen, how wrong you were to distrust us, you have our words in proof of it. Will you not now believe me?'

But Penelope gave him no answer, for she knew that he was lying.

When she did not reply, Eurymachus went on, 'Let it comfort your mind and make you of good cheer to know that there lives no man—no, nor shall he ever live—who shall do Telemachus the slightest hurt, while I yet breathe. I swear to you, Queen Penelope, that were any man so rash and so evilly disposed as to seek to harm your son, very quickly would his blood be flowing on the ground, and his base life be leaving him, thanks to my good spear. For of all men in Ithaca, young Telemachus is the dearest to me, both for himself alone and for his fair mother's sake. Believe me, I implore you, good Penelope, for I speak the truth.'

Again she did not answer him, and Eurymachus sought to persuade her further with his flattering tongue. 'And even if it were not reason enough, that I should cherish him for his own sake and for his mother's, could I forget his father, good Odysseus? For he was always kind to me when I was a little child, and often would I come to this very hall, running eagerly to see him, in the old days before he wedded you and brought you to his house. And always did he welcome me with friendliness, talking to me as one talks to a child one loves, and asking me about my boyish games and pleasures. In the feasting he would set me upon his knee and give me meat and bread from off his plate, and let me sip wine out of the king's own cup. Oh, fair Queen Penelope, if not for the sake of anyone else, then for the sake of the memory of good Odysseus, would I hold dear his son. For Odysseus was a fine man whom I loved well, and the greatest pity it is, that Ithaca will never see him home again.'

At the mention of her husband, Penelope's eyes filled with tears, and fearing she could no longer contain her grief, she turned and went from the hall, going up once more to her apartments with her handmaidens. There upon her couch she lay and wept, remembering Odysseus.

But Eurymachus sat down, and turning to Antinous who sprawled beside him, said, 'It is with all speed that Telemachus must die, for while he lives no one of us has a chance to win the queen. The wretched youth has poisoned her against us.'

Early the next morning Telemachus told the swineherd that he was returning to the town to his mother. 'For,' he said, 'I fear that she will not be satisfied until she has seen for herself that I am safe and well.'

'Dear prince,' said Eumaeus, 'you will take good care for your life, I beg, and trust none of the suitors.'

'I shall be cautious, never fear, Eumaeus, but now I must be gone. Do you come after me later in the day, bringing with you the stranger. For he and I talked together yesterday when you were with my mother, and it seems that he will not be content until he has tried his fortune in the town and seen for himself the home of Odysseus, whom he knew. So come to the house, both of you, and I shall be waiting there.'

He bade Eumaeus farewell with affection, and said to Odysseus, 'Stranger, I shall expect to see you later.' But unseen by the swineherd he clasped his father's hand and smiled at him, whispering, 'Good luck be with you.' Then he was gone, walking quickly down the hill-side.

When he came to the house of Odysseus it was still early and the suitors had not yet arrived. The first person he saw when he entered the hall was old Eurycleia. She was spreading fleecy rugs and woven cloths over the chairs to make all comfortable for the wooers when they should arrive, muttering to herself as she worked, and grumbling that she should have to toil for wicked men when her good master was far from home.

'Greetings, nurse,' called Telemachus from the great doorway, and with a cry of joy she dropped the coverlets she held and went to him.

'My dear child, I had thought never to see you again, and when the swineherd brought your message yesterday, it was almost more joy than my old bones could bear,' she said, kissing him; and then could speak no more, for she was weeping for happiness.

One of Penelope's handmaidens came into the hall and saw him there, and called out to the other maids, 'Prince Telemachus is back,' and instantly they came running and gathered round him, greeting him and asking questions. Penelope heard the bustle and excitement and came down herself to find out what had befallen.

Telemachus saw her standing in the doorway at the far end of the hall, and leaving the women, he ran down the room to her and took her in his arms. 'Dear mother,' he said, 'were you very troubled for me?'

'My son,' she said, and her tears flowed fast, 'I was afraid that I should never see you again. You are all that I have left to me since your father sailed for Troy. For twenty years you have been my only comfort. If those cruel men had killed you, I think that I should have died from grief.'

Telemachus kissed her and laughed. 'But dry your eyes now, mother, for I am home, and safely. This is no time for weeping.'

Penelope smiled at him. 'In truth, I have been so afraid, and now am so overjoyed, I know not whether I should laugh or cry. But you must tell me, what news was there of your father in Pylos?'

Seeing the anxious longing in her eyes, Telemachus had not the heart to see her further wounded, and he was afraid that if he spoke longer to her, he might betray his father's secret and perhaps spoil all their plans. So quickly he said, 'I beg you to excuse me now, dear mother, but I must go to the assembly place to speak with our old friends and father's, good Mentor and the others, and tell them I am home. For though they knew not of the suitors' plot, rumour of some danger to me may have disturbed them. Besides, there is a stranger, one Theoclymenus, who seeks refuge here in Ithaca from his enemies. He sailed with us from Pylos, and I gave him in charge of Peiraeus until such time as I could bring him here. I must go now and fetch him, that we may make him welcome in our house. When I return I will tell you all that passed at Pylos and in Sparta. Meanwhile, dearest mother, go to your room and pray to all the gods that they may be with us, for I believe that soon will come a day of reckoning for your suitors.'

He left her wondering at his words, but hardly daring to hope that they meant more than just that he, as she did, still waited patiently and with devoted confidence for Odysseus to come home.

As Telemachus passed through the courtyard on his way to the town, he met certain of the suitors coming through the gates. They crowded round him with fair words, and questions as to the success of his mission to King Nestor; but with no more than a brief greeting he hurried past them, whistling to him his two favourite hounds who had come into the courtyard on hearing his voice. Patting the dogs, and running with them as if in play, he was able to avoid the more persistent of the suitors who were eager to learn where he was going, and he went on alone towards the town.

'He is going to the place of assembly,' said one of them. 'Let us follow him lest he speak against us in our absence.' And some of them hurried after him.

But once at the assembly place, Telemachus again avoided them, and sought out among those present the old friends of his father, good Mentor who had stood up to speak for him when he had accused the wooers before he sailed to Pylos, and old Halitherses, who had known his father as a boy, and several others.

They greeted him warmly and asked him many questions concerning all that had befallen him on his journey; and he sat down beside them and answered willingly, telling them of King Nestor and Menelaus and Helen. And all the while the suitors watched him carefully to see if he should at any time stand up before the men of Ithaca and denounce them for their crimes. But Telemachus had other plans, and talked only of his travels.

After an hour or so there came to him Peiraeus, with Theoclymenus by his side. 'Greetings, Telemachus,' Peiraeus said. 'The gifts you left with me are safely in my home, would you that I should send them to your father's house?'

'Peiraeus, my friend,' replied Telemachus, 'all things are not well between me and my mother's wooers. Should any evil come to me from them, it would be my wish that you, who proved yourself so good a comrade on the voyage to Pylos, should have for yourself those gifts that King Menelaus gave me, rather than that the suitors should divide the treasures among themselves with never a friend of mine there to forbid them. So keep the gifts for me until I may call my father's house my home again, and not the gathering-place of all my enemies.' Then turning to Theoclymenus, he said, 'But if you have a mind to come with me, good friend, my mother and I will make you very welcome. Unless,' he smiled, 'you would prefer not to meet her wooers. For they are not men one would chose to meet, I can assure you.'

But Theoclymenus laughed and replied, 'I am ready to meet even your mother's wicked suitors, so long as I am safe from my own enemies. And I think, Telemachus, that those men who waste your possessions in your father's house will not do it unchecked much longer. That is my belief, and as I told you, I have some skill in prophecy.'

So Telemachus went back to Odysseus' house once more, and Theoclymenus went with him. And there Eurycleia set food and wine for them upon a table in a quiet corner of the hall, while Penelope brought her spinning and sat close by, to hear all her son's adventures.

He told her everything that had passed between him and Nestor, and of King Menelaus' splendid palace, and of beautiful Queen Helen; keeping till the last the tidings of

Odysseus that Menelaus had had from the Old Man of the Sea. 'At least he was alive when Menelaus heard those words, and it is likely he is living yet, and, dearest mother, soon he may be home, if the gods are good to us,' he said, thinking while he spoke of how before long Odysseus would be entering the hall with the good swineherd, Eumaeus.

But Penelope wiped away a tear, and her spinning lay idle on her lap. She shook her head. 'How shall he break free from the snare of an immortal nymph?' she said. 'He never will come home.'

'With the help of the gods all things are possible, and I know that there is an immortal god with us, aiding us, even this very day,' said Telemachus, longing to ease her grief by telling her the truth.

Theoclymenus leant forward, 'Good queen,' he said, 'believe me when I tell you that all things will come to pass favourably for you and for your family. Even now is your husband Odysseus on his way home, and soon he will be standing in this very hall. I cannot tell you how I know this, but only that I am sure of it, and my soothsaying has ever been proved true in the past.'

Telemachus looked at his guest with admiration, marvelling at the man's foreknowledge of what was, as yet, a secret known only to him and to his father.

'May what you speak be true, good Theoclymenus,' said Penelope, 'so shall you ever be honoured by me and mine.'

But at that moment Medon the herald went into the courtyard where the suitors were disporting themselves with games and contests of skill, and called them in to their midday meal, and Penelope retired to her own rooms.

XVII

Odysseus goes Home

IN the afternoon Odysseus and the swineherd set out for the town. As they made their way down the hill-path and were nearing the outskirts of the city, at a spot where there was a spring from which many of the towns-folk fetched their water, they fell in with Melanthius, who kept Odysseus' goats on a farm beyond the hills. With the help of two of his herdsmen he was driving a flock of goats to Odysseus' house that the suitors might have plentiful meat for their feasting. And glad he was to do it, for the suitors were men to his liking, extravagant, reckless, and impudent. He served them well, and looked forward to the day when one of them should be married to his mistress and he might gain a higher position in the household.

Melanthius had stopped to chat with some women who were drawing water, and when he saw the swineherd approach with a ragged old beggarman, he came forward, and looking Odysseus up and down with a contemptuous air, said, 'Indeed, our friend Eumaeus keeps fitting company, one cringing whiner with another. Have you really the impertinence, Eumaeus, to bring another beggar to the house to eat good food meant for his betters, and trouble with his demands for alms the noble suitors? You would do better to give him to me, to sweep my yard and fetch fodder for the kids and help in many ways. I should soon find work for him to do, I promise you. But then I have no doubt he does not wish to earn his keep, preferring to wander from town to town and house to house, with some unlikely story of his misfortunes, relying on the kindness of others. I know that manner of man, and we want none in our house. If he shows his ugly face there, I hope the noble suitors will give him all he deserves and fling him out into the road again speedily.'

And with that he aimed a kick at Odysseus, who, however, stood firm, wondering whether he should strike down the insolent wretch with his staff, or whether he should hold his peace and wait for his revenge until his more important task of destroying the wooers was accomplished.

'For shame, Melanthius, to strike an old man,' cried Eumaeus. 'Your ways have grown insufferable since the suitors took to favouring you. Would that the immortal gods might hear my prayers and send our master, King Odysseus, home. In his days no needy wanderer was turned from the door, and in his days no servant would have dared to speak as you have done.'

'Just hear how the swineherd snaps. He is like a snarling dog,' jeered Melanthius. 'You can cease your praying, Eumaeus, you fool, for you only waste your time, the master never will come back, he is lying dead, somewhere far away from Ithaca. And my only wish is that Prince Telemachus were lying beside his father. A happy day would it be for us should that prim youth die suddenly.' And with that he called to his men to hurry up the goats, and strode away after them shouting at the beasts.

But Odysseus and Eumaeus followed slowly and without speech. Eumaeus in embarrassment because he could think of no words to say that might soothe his guest's feelings, hurt by the goatherd's discourtesy, and considering himself to be in a certain measure responsible for what had occurred, for he and Melanthius were old enemies, and railed most times they met. While Odysseus was silent because he was at last approaching his home again, after nearly twenty years; but not in the way he had dreamed of, as a king, proud and happy, clad in clean and shining raiment, escorted by his people, to see his wife and son waiting for him at the gates with smiling faces; but as a tattered old beggar, bent and aged, leaning on a staff and wearing dirty rags, led only by a swineherd, while his wife did not even know that he was coming, and his son might not acknowledge him.

Close by the gates Odysseus paused and was the first to break the silence. 'My friend,' he said, 'had I been asked, I should have said this to be the house of Odysseus. Am I right?'

'It is indeed my master's house,' replied Eumaeus. 'You have guessed well.'

'It seemed to me to be the house of a king,' said Odysseus. 'See how high and strong the walls are, and how great the gates. The courtyard, too, is spacious, and the house itself is large and lofty, even that little I can see of it from here, beyond the half-open gates.'

'It is a wide and stately house, well fitted to be the home of a mighty and noble man such as my master was. But now is it filled with the evil thoughts and unseemly revelry of those who have no right to sit beneath its roof,' said Eumaeus. He paused for a moment, lost in bitter reflection, then went on, 'Good stranger, we must now decide whether we shall go together into the great hall, or whether you would prefer that I should go in before you, that you may follow me to try your fortune with the wooers, if they will give you food or not. Or perchance you would go first, alone, and have me come after you? For if any sees you standing for long at the gates, he may drive you away with stones and harsh words.'

Odysseus smiled. 'Full used am I to harsh words and blows, no beggar may evade them. So go you in first, good swineherd, and I will follow you.'

'Let it be as you wish, stranger,' said Eumaeus, and made to pass into the courtyard.

At the gates there lay an old hound, dozing in the sunshine. He had once been a fine animal, full of strength and speed, but now he was old and neglected. In the very year that Odysseus had left home to go to Troy, he had bred and trained him, naming him Argus. He had shown promise of being the finest hound that his master had ever had, but Odysseus had not seen the fulfilment of that promise, for he had left Argus barely more than a puppy when he had sailed from Ithaca. But in spite of all the years that had passed since then, Odysseus thought that he knew the hound, and he spoke to Eumaeus, 'It is a strange thing to see a fine hound such as this lying neglected at the gate. He is old now, but he looks as though he must once have been swift and unerring in the chase.'

Argus heard and recognized his master's voice, and opened his eyes, pricking up his ears. He moved his head a little and wagged his tail. The eyes of Odysseus filled with tears, and he turned away his face from the swineherd.

'He was indeed a fine animal,' said Eumaeus, 'and my master trained him himself. He was once the fleetest of foot and the keenest on the scent of all the hounds in Ithaca. But now that he is past his hunting days the servants never care for him, though my good master would not have forgotten him in his old age. Truly, servants grow neglectful in the master's absence, and in King Odysseus' house nothing is as it should be.'

Argus tried to rise and go to Odysseus, but he was too old and feeble, and the effort was too much for him; and he dropped his head and died.

'I will go on into the house,' said Eumaeus, 'come after me as quickly as you may.' And he went across the courtyard and under the porch.

Odysseus stepped over to Argus and bent to pat him, but he saw that the old hound was dead. He brushed away his tears, and then smiled a little, gratefully, as he reflected that, after all, he had not come quite unwelcomed to his home. Then he crossed the courtyard to the porch, and entered once more, after twenty years, his own house, an aged, tattered beggar bent over a stick.

In the great hall the suitors had gathered together for their evening meal and their talking and laughter echoed to the roof. Odysseus sat down upon the threshold and waited, looking around him carefully at those assembled there. He saw Eumaeus carrying forward a stool to place it near Telemachus who leant across to speak to him. He noticed, too, Melanthius, the goatherd, sitting close to Eurymachus, drinking and laughing with him. For Eurymachus was the one of all the suitors whom Melanthius believed most likely to win the queen, and therefore he ever sought out his company, with an eye to future benefits.

Odysseus had not been waiting long before Telemachus caught sight of him. Quickly he gave Eumaeus a loaf of bread and a platter of meat and bade him take them to his father. 'The stranger has come,' he said. 'Go, give him food, and tell him, if he wishes more, to beg it of the wooers. For shame and an empty purse are but ill-matched companions, and modesty takes a poor man nowhere.' So he spoke that his father might have a chance to see for himself what manner of men the wooers were.

The swineherd brought the food over to Odysseus at once, and told him what Telemachus had said.

'May the gods bless the good prince,' said Odysseus; and Eumaeus returned to his seat.

Odysseus ate the bread and meat, and when it was all eaten, he rose and went among the suitors to see if they would spare him more. He began with the man on the left of the room, working his way round the semicircle of feasters which ended with Antinous on the very right. He held out his hand before each man and muttered a word or two of appeal, in the very way a real beggar would have done. Most of them gave him something, a scrap of meat or a piece of bread, and a few of them asked among each other where he had come from, for they had not seen him in the house before.

'I can tell you where he comes from,' called out Melanthius, who had heard the question, 'and who brought him here, for I saw the swineherd leading him to the town. But who he is I have no idea.'

Antinous caught his words and frowned, for he cared not for Eumaeus, because the swineherd loved his master whose possessions Antinous coveted. 'Swineherd,' he shouted across the hall, 'we have enough beggars in Ithaca already, why did you bring us another to molest us at our feasts? Are you so eager to waste your master's food?' He sneered, 'You are ever speaking in his praise, and whining that he comes not home, so that I should have thought you would have shown more care for his goods.'

'Lord Antinous,' replied Eumaeus, 'you may come of a noble family, but your words are base. No one could turn away from his door an unfortunate wanderer whose very livelihood depended on charity. It is a duty of all more fortunate men to help such needy folk. But you, Lord Antinous, have always been harsh, not only to beggars, but to all the slaves of my dear master, and to me above all others. Yet can I bear it, so long as our gracious Queen Penelope and the young prince are kind.'

Telemachus interrupted him. 'No, Eumaeus,' he said, 'do not give angry words to Antinous, or let him provoke you by his gibes. For it is ever his pleasure to stir up strife and quarrelling with an ill-intentioned speech.' He turned to Antinous and said with irony, 'I thank you, Antinous, for your fatherly care for my goods, in that you will not let me waste a few crumbs on a beggar. But I do not grudge it to him, rather would I see you give liberally of that which is not your own to give. Come, Antinous, help yourself to my father's food, bestow it, and earn the thanks of a beggar. Or do you prefer to keep for yourself all that you take from this house?'

'You are again at your boasting, young Telemachus,' said Antinous with fury. 'I had hoped that we should have been spared more of it, but it seems we are unlucky. As for your old beggarman, I can tell you that if all my comrades were to give him what I should like to offer, the rogue would keep from this house for three months or more.' And as he spoke he picked up the footstool from beneath his feet, and with it threatened Odysseus.

The other suitors laughed, but for all that they seemed not to heed his words, for they gave Odysseus food in answer to his pleading, down to the very one who sat to the right of Antinous.

And then Odysseus stood before Antinous himself and said, 'Lord, you seem to me to be the noblest of all present, in pride and bearing like a king. Do then give me a gift as your companions have done, and let it be a greater gift than theirs, even as you are the greater man. And in return I shall speak your praises in every land where I may wander. For know that I, too, was once a rich man, with great possessions of my own; and so long as I had enough, would I give to all who asked. But I came to misfortune and am now even as you see me today, a poor and homeless wanderer dependent on the kindness of good men like yourself.'

'Spare us the tale of your misfortunes,' said Antinous, 'and begone. Or else you will regret the gift I give you.' And he turned away contemptuously and called for more wine.

Odysseus looked at him. 'It seems I was mistaken in my judgement,' he said, 'and you are not the man you appear to be from your outward show. I wonder,' he went on with a mocking smile, 'since you are so miserly with other people's goods, what would you give of your own possessions to a beggar in your own house? Not a single grain of salt, I fear.'

Jumping to his feet Antinous seized the footstool and flung it at Odysseus, saying, 'Now begone, you shameless wretch that dare to speak so to me. You heeded not my warning to go in peace, so now shall you be driven forth.'

But Odysseus stood firm beneath the blow and gave no answer, though his heart was filled with wrath. Instead he went back to the door and sat down once more upon the threshold.

And a few among the wooers said to Antinous, 'Was it not rash, Antinous, to strike the stranger? What if he should prove to be one of the immortal gods come down to earth to see how we mortals live? For, remember, we know nothing of whence he comes, save only that the swineherd brought him here.'

But Antinous only scowled at them and drank his wine and cared not for their words. And Telemachus clenched his fists and swore to be avenged for the cowardly blow given to his father.

One of the servants, going through the door at the end of the hall to fetch more food, met a handmaid of Penelope going about her tasks, and told her of how Antinous had struck a harmless beggar who had been brought to the house by Eumaeus. The woman later told Penelope, who grew angry, crying out, 'So may the arrogant Antinous himself one day be struck down.'

'May the gods hear your prayer, mistress,' said the old nurse, Eurycleia, fervently.

'In truth,' said Penelope, 'out of my suitors he is the most hateful of all. What a pass things have come to if in Odysseus' house his own wife and son cannot shield from insult and violence a poor beggar.' She called to one of her serving-maids, saying, 'Go now and bid Eumaeus the swineherd come and speak with me, for I would ask him of the stranger.'

When Eumaeus had come to her, Penelope questioned him concerning Odysseus, who he was and whence he had come. And when the swineherd had answered her, she said, 'Tell him, good Eumaeus, that I would speak with him, for from your account of him he seems an honest and a much-travelled man, and perchance he could give me news of my husband.'

'Indeed, mistress,' replied the swineherd, 'he is a fine talker. Three days I had him with me in my house, and yet all his tales were not told, nor do I think they ever would be, though one had him at one's side for three months, or even years, for there seems to be no end to his adventures. And of my master he often spoke, saying that he had fought with him at Troy.'

'Go quickly, Eumaeus,' said Penelope eagerly, 'go quickly and bring him to me.'

So the swineherd returned to the hall and gave

Penelope's message to Odysseus. But Odysseus answered, 'I am afraid of the anger of the suitors, if they see that the queen is kind to me. Therefore beg her to wait until they have gone to their homes tonight, and then let her ask me what she will about her husband, and I shall gladly answer her.'

When Penelope heard from Eumaeus this reply, she said, 'Truly, that stranger is a wise man, and in a little space of time has he seen clearly how things stand in our house. I will go down to the hall myself tonight when the suitors are gone, and speak with him.'

Eumaeus then went to Telemachus to bid him good night. 'I must return to my swine,' he said. 'But take good care of yourself, my prince,' he added in a whisper, 'for you are among your enemies, they stand thick on every side.'

'Good night, Eumaeus,' replied Telemachus. 'Come early in the morning, and see how we have fared.'

And with a kindly word of farewell to Odysseus as he passed him in the doorway, the swineherd returned to his farm, glad to be away from the suitors once again, but disturbed for his young master's safety.

Soon after this the suitors fell to merry-making with song and dance, and Phemius the minstrel played long for them; while Odysseus sat upon the threshold and watched all that went on, warily.

Now there was in Ithaca a rogue named Irus, a fat, greedy man, whose trade it was to go from house to house seeking food and drink and entertainment, posing as a man whom fortune had misused, though the truth was that he had ever preferred a life of idleness and would not have had it otherwise. He would sometimes run errands when he was bidden, but mostly when there was any work to be done, Irus was not there. He was well known to the suitors who found his company amusing, and was even favoured by Antinous, who otherwise seldom encouraged beggars.

This Irus now came to Odysseus' house, and finding Odysseus by the door, he made to fling him out from his own home. 'Away, old man,' he said, 'that place is mine. Go speedily, before I have to chase you out. I am sure the noble suitors will be glad to see no more of you.'

'My friend,' said Odysseus, 'I grudge you nothing that the queen's suitors may give to you, and I would not take anything that was yours by right. But this house is large, and the threshold is wide enough for the two of us. Come, be peaceable and let us agree, for though I am an old man I am still good for a fight, and I shall defend myself if you provoke me with your fists.'

Irus laughed scornfully. 'How could you fight with a younger man? Your boasts are idle. Get you gone, or else stand up that I may show the noble suitors how I can protect my rights.'

Antinous heard his words and laughed. He leapt to his feet, his face flushed and his legs a little unsteady from the wine that he had drunk. 'My friends,' he said, 'one of the immortal gods has sent us a rare entertainment. Irus and the stranger are quarrelling together. Let us set them on to fight and see which of them is the better man, fat Irus or the old ragged fool.'

Gleefully they all agreed; and Telemachus hated them more than he had ever hated them before.

Antinous moved over to the hearth, and with a hand that still held a wine-cup, pointed to the fire. 'Here at the fire, my friends, we have some fine black puddings cooking for our supper. I say that we should give to the winner of this contest his choice among them tonight. And more than that, I say that we should give him the freedom of our table, that he may always feast with us, and we shall allow no other beggars in the house.'

His words were met with cheers and laughter. 'It will be a mighty jest,' the other suitors said.

Odysseus rose. 'Noble lords,' he said, 'I will undertake to fight only if you will promise me that no one of you, eager to see his favourite Irus win, will strike me down. Let me have only Irus matched against me, I beg of you, for I am an old man.'

To this they all agreed and gave their word, and Telemachus cried out, 'Stranger, if you should be the victor in this combat, I swear to you that if any man here dare fall upon you, he shall find me fighting at your side.'

The suitors crowded round to see the sport, and Odysseus put aside his old leather jerkin and tucked up his ragged tunic round his thighs.

'He has a fine pair of legs, for all that he is an old man,' said the wooers to one another. 'And his shoulders are broad enough, under those rags of his.' And straightway there were many among them who said, 'In spite of his age, I have a fancy that the stranger will soon lay Irus on the floor.'

And Irus heard them and was afraid, for he was no fighter, and had only dared to flout Odysseus thinking him to be a weak old man and spiritless; and he tried to slip away unseen from the hall. But he was prevented, and with force he was led back and ranged opposite Odysseus.

Odysseus and Irus put up their hands and circled round each other for a few moments, urged on by the suitors, who called out, some for Irus and some for the stranger. Encouraged by the men who called his name, Irus struck the first blow and caught Odysseus on the shoulder. At once Odysseus replied with a mighty stroke upon the side of Irus' head, and the fat rogue fell down to the ground and lay there groaning.

The wooers rocked with laughter and drank more wine in celebration of the victory, while Odysseus dragged Irus by the foot out of the hall and across to the courtyard gates. There he left him, propped against the wall, and returned to the suitors. They greeted him with cheers and laughter, and bade him sit and eat with them. Antinous handed him the largest of the black puddings, and the others brought him bread and drink, and pledged him with many draughts of wine. 'Better fortune to you, stranger, in the days to come.'

XVIII

Odysseus speaks with his Wife

WHILE the suitors made merry in his house, with Odysseus in their midst, his thoughts full of irony at the strange situation, it came to the mind of Penelope to go down to the great hall and show herself once more to her wooers and bid her son spend less time in their company. Adorned and fair she left her rooms and descended the stairs with two of her maidens. They opened for her the door at the far end of the hall, and she passed through and stood close by the threshold with a maid on either side. When the suitors saw her they ceased their clamour and drinking, and stared at her; and never had she seemed to them more lovely.

And Odysseus looked up and saw her standing there, in

a robe of many-pleated white linen, with a purple veil over her hair.

'Telemachus,' she said, 'when you were a child your deeds were ever governed by the knowledge of what it is right to do. But of late it seems that you have changed. Perhaps it is because of the company you keep.' She glanced around at the suitors with contempt, and went on, 'It was not well done to let a stranger be insulted and mistreated in our house, and I am indeed ashamed that such a thing should have come to pass.'

Odysseus watched her as she stood there speaking, and thought how in twenty years she had not really changed. 'She is older,' he said to himself, 'how could she be otherwise? For now she is a woman, and I left her a young bride. Yet she is still the same Penelope.' And seeing her there, he knew at last, that in spite of his disguise and the suitors and the dangers he was about to face, he was truly home. And his heart felt great content.

Telemachus answered her quietly. 'Dear mother, I do not wonder at your anger in this matter. In my heart I know what it is right and what it is wrong to do, even as I did when I was but a child. Yet I am not master in my own father's house, and all things here are not ordered as I could wish.' He went over to her, adding in a low voice, 'The servants may have told you how they set Irus and the stranger on to fight with one another. But the combat fell not out as they expected, for the stranger showed himself to be by far the better man, and Irus sits, witless, beyond the gates. Oh, mother, how I wish that all your suitors were ranged alongside him, and our home were ours once more.'

While Telemachus yet spoke to her, Eurymachus called out, 'Fair Queen Penelope, you are more beautiful tonight than ever I remember you. If all the men of Greece might see you now, then tomorrow would you have many more suitors than we are, and the house would not be large enough to hold us all.'

Gravely Penelope answered him, 'Eurymachus, the immortal gods took all the joy and comeliness from me on the day my husband sailed for Troy. If he might but return to me again, then indeed might I seem fair. For the happy have always a beauty of their own, even though their countenance may be ill favoured. Hard it is for a woman to lose her beloved husband and be forced to choose another lord and leave her home. But harder it is when her wooers are such as you and your companions, who are ever in that home of hers, eating and drinking and wasting her son's inheritance. Shame on you all, this is no way to win a wife.'

Antinous spoke up, 'Sweet Penelope, I shall not move from this place until you have chosen the best out of us all to be your husband, and all my comrades are agreed with me in this. And here I drink to you in pledge of my word.' And he drained another cupful of red wine.

But Penelope drew the folds of her purple veil across her face and turned away from them and left the room, followed by her women. And the suitors called for lights, for evening was come on.

Three braziers set with torches were lighted at the fire and placed about the hall, and a few of the serving-maids stood beside them to see that they did not go out or weaken, keeping them fed with faggots; laughing meanwhile with the suitors, calling to them and answering jest with jest; until Odysseus grew annoyed to see them spend their time thus.

'You idle wenches,' he said, 'go back to your mistress, that she may find you work to do, and I will tend the lights for you.'

The maids laughed at his words, and with a toss of her head, one of them answered him pertly, 'Foolish old man, why do you come here to plague us all? Go, find shelter for the night in some peasant's hovel, under a roof more fitted to your rags.'

Angry to think that a servant in his house should speak so to one she believed to be a homeless wanderer, Odysseus said, 'You shameless creature, to speak such words to an old man. Beware lest I tell Prince Telemachus of your impertinence. Now go as I bade you, and leave me to mind the lights.'

Afraid at his threat, the serving-maids ran from the hall, and Odysseus was left to keep the burning braziers replenished with dry wood.

Then Eurymachus taunted Odysseus, saying, 'Old man, shall I find you work upon my farm that you may earn an honest living, gathering stones to build walls between my fields or planting out young saplings? Or are you rather one of those who prefer to live in idleness on the gifts that others give you?'

Odysseus answered him, 'Indeed, Eurymachus, I wish that you and I, each with a sharp scythe in his hands, could be matched against each other from dawn to dusk in the season of haymaking; or that we were each in a good-sized field with a plough and two strong oxen to draw it. I warrant that my hay would be sooner reaped than yours, and that I could plough a straighter furrow. You would not scorn me, could you see me at work. Or better yet, were you to watch me in the press of battle, with my armour on and my good sword in my hand, putting my foes to flight, you would not jeer at me for long. But you have grown insolent, Eurymachus, and think yourself a mighty man, because you spend your days among those who are even weaker and of less account than you.'

Eurymachus grew angry and forgot his usual smooth-speaking ways. 'The wine you have drunk has gone to your head,' he said, 'or perhaps your defeat of Irus has made you proud, for else you would not dare to speak so to me.' And as Antinous had done, he picked up a footstool and flung it at Odysseus. But Odysseus stepped aside, and the stool struck a servant who was carrying a bowl of wine, and with a clatter of metal all the wine was spilt upon the floor. And instantly the suitors were making an outcry and complaining, and there was an uproar in the hall.

Telemachus rose, and shouting to make himself heard above the clamour, he said, 'Surely you have all of you drunk too much of my father's good wine, that you disturb my house with your rioting. Go now to your own homes and sleep, leaving me in peace.'

They were all amazed at his words, that he should have dared to speak so boldly to them, but they said to one another, 'Perhaps it is best that we go, sleep will be welcome to us, and tomorrow we can feast again.' And when they had each taken a last cupful of wine, they went from the hall to their own homes, peaceably enough.

Now, it was the custom to keep certain weapons in the

hall for when they might be wanted; long spears and javelins propped beside the pillars, so that they were ready for hunting or javelin-throwing contests such as the suitors were wont to hold in the courtyard. There were, also, upon the wall, swords and shields hanging, in case they should be needed by someone going on a journey, that the traveller might protect himself from robbers.

Odysseus considered these weapons, how the suitors could snatch them up and arm themselves when he and Telemachus fell upon them; and though two well-armed men might prevail against a hundred who had, with which to defend themselves, only the swords they wore, those two would have but little chance against a hundred men with spears and javelins to throw, and shields to hold before their bodies.

So as soon as the last of the suitors had departed, and Odysseus was alone in the hall with his son, he said, 'These weapons must we put by in the armoury where lie the other arms, or the suitors will use them to our hurt. And if any should observe and ask questions of you as to why this thing has been done, say that you have laid them away because they needed polishing, having become grimy with the smoke from the fire; or that you feared that in the evenings, when they have drunk much wine, some of the suitors might fall to quarrelling, and it were best that no weapons should be by. Leave only for yourself and for me, two swords, two spears and a shield for each, and place them where you may reach them easily when they are needed. Come now, and let us hide the rest away.'

So Telemachus sent for Eurycleia and asked her for the key of the store-room which she kept, and together he and his father laid by the weapons in the armoury, alongside the others that were there. And many journeys did they make to and from the great hall through the door half-way down the side wall, along the passage to the high chamber where the treasure of Odysseus lay, their arms full of swords and shields or bunches of long spears, observed of none at their task.

When only the two swords and spears and shields that Odysseus and Telemachus would need for themselves remained in the hall, Odysseus said to his son, 'Go now and sleep while I wait here, for your mother has sent word that she would speak with me.'

So Telemachus bade his father good night and went alone to his own room; his mind so full, pondering the happenings of the day, and wondering what might befall on the morrow, that he feared he could not rest; but nevertheless, in spite of all, he soon fell into a sound sleep.

Then came the servants to clear away the cups and dishes and the tables which the suitors had used for their feast, and to make all tidy and orderly in the hall. Then, too, Penelope came down from her apartments with her maids, who set for her beside the fire her own chair of wood inlaid with a pattern worked in silver and ivory.

One of the servants who was favoured by the wooers, seeing Odysseus still waiting in the hall, spoke discourteously to him, saying, 'Old stranger, is it not time that you were gone from the house? Surely you have had your fill of food and wine? There is no more for you, so begone, before you are driven forth.'

Angrily Odysseus answered, 'It is more seemly to be patient and kindly to those less fortunate than oneself.

Some day you too may meet with ill luck and find yourself a wretched outcast, with no kind mistress or young master to give you protection.'

Penelope, too, heard the unkind words, and she rebuked the servant, saying, 'Be silent now, and suffer the stranger to remain in peace. You are not so insolent with my suitors who come here unbidden, as you are with my son's invited guests. What an ill thing it is when the servants think to rule in the house. But beware, impertinent one, lest even yet your master should come home.' And Penelope called Odysseus over to her, and her maids set a chair for him, beside the fire, close to hers.

'Tell me, stranger, what is your name and where is your home?'

'Good queen,' replied Odysseus, 'my story is an unhappy one, ask me no more to relate it, for the remembrance of all that has befallen me lies heavily on my sad heart, and I would not speak of it. Ask me of anything else that you will, and I shall answer truly. But ask me not to tell you of my sufferings, for I could not speak of them without tears, and it is not seemly that a guest should weep and wail in another's house. I know that you will be understanding in this, good queen, for the fame of your virtues has travelled far, even beyond the shores of Ithaca.'

'No, stranger,' Penelope said sadly, 'that is not so, for all my virtues of beauty and of character died when my dear husband sailed to Troy. Since then I have been but the shadow of a woman, a poor pale creature groping through life, ever grieving and ever fearful, as a woman must be who has lost the husband she loved and has no lord to protect her.' She sighed. 'And now am I beset by suitors who would wed me and take me from my home. For three years have I kept them waiting for an answer, while I ever hoped Odysseus might return. I have tricked them and deceived them, trying to gain time, but at last the day has come when I can no longer delay my choice. My son is now a man and should rule in his own house, but so long as my wooers remain in his halls, defying his authority and eating his food, he never will be master in his home. And since here they have sworn to remain until I take from among their number a new lord, then must I now make my decision. But any husband that I take will be without a doubt far inferior to my dear Odysseus, and that is a hard fate for any woman to face.'

'Your husband was in truth an excellent man,' said Odysseus. 'I remember how once he came to my house on his way to Troy. I was in better fortune then and could offer him entertainment with a willing heart. Twelve days did he and his men remain in my home, and many were the hours in which Odysseus and I talked together. Truly, he was a goodly man.'

Penelope wept at his lying tale, for she thought he spoke the truth and she was sad to think that this stranger had seen and talked to Odysseus after he had gone from her, perhaps for ever. But though she believed the story, she had been deceived by other tales before, and so cautiously she tested him. 'Tell me, good stranger, that I may be sure you speak the truth, what my Odysseus looked like when he came to your house. What garments was he wearing?'

'Gracious queen, it is many years since I saw him, and it is not easy to remember such things. But I will tell you all that my memory can recall for me. He wore a soft, close-fitting tunic, woven of some shining thread, and over it a purple cloak, fastened upon the shoulder with a golden brooch fashioned in the likeness of a hound bringing down a deer. A curious brooch it was, and therefore can I see it now with my mind's eye.'

Thus did Odysseus describe the clothes that he had worn when he had left his home to sail to Troy; and Penelope remembered them and her tears flowed fast.

'Now, indeed, stranger, am I certain that you speak the truth and I will trust you in all things. For it was I who gave him the garments that you saw him wear. The cloak I had woven for him myself, and the brooch I chose out from my jewel-casket, for it was a favourite one of mine.' She paused a moment, then went on with a deep sigh, 'How sad it is to talk of one whom we shall never see again. Good stranger, you must pardon my distress.'

'Gracious queen, it is most fitting that a wife should grieve for a husband who is dead, but I would bid you cease your weeping, for Odysseus is alive. I swear to you that very soon he will be home again, and you and your son may rejoice at his return. Believe me, noble lady, for I speak the truth.'

Penelope shook her head. 'I wish that I might believe you, stranger,' she said sadly, 'but I am afraid that Odysseus never will come back, he has been gone too long, and I must now accept my fate and make my choice from among my suitors. But it grows late, let me not keep you longer from your rest with the recital of my sorrows.' And she called to her maidens to prepare him a bed in the vestibule, as befitted an honoured guest, and sent for old Eurycleia and bade her bring a basin of water to wash the stranger's feet; and the old woman came hurrying with a brazen bowl, a towel of white linen, and two ewers with water, both hot and cold.

And even as she came towards him Odysseus remembered the scar upon his leg where once he had been wounded by a boar, while out hunting when he was but a youth, and he knew that his old nurse would recognize it if she saw it; so he turned away towards the shadows, hoping that in the dim light her old eyes would not notice anything.

Eurycleia laid the basin at his feet, and looking at him closely, said, 'Never in all my life have I heard a voice so like my dear master's as yours. You are many years older than he would have been had he lived to return to his house, but if I closed my eyes to listen to you speak, I should think he had come back.'

Odysseus answered her quickly, 'Indeed, good woman, many others than you have marked the likeness and said the same to me.'

The old nurse knelt before him and poured water into the basin and took hold of his foot, and at once she saw the scar. With a cry she started back and the bowl tipped over and all the water was spilt upon the floor.

'You are my dear Lord Odysseus,' gasped Eurycleia, and she looked towards Penelope to tell her the glad news.

But swiftly Odysseus grasped her by the shoulder, 'Hush, nurse, would you see me slain by the suitors? Keep silent, I charge you. For I must first destroy those wicked men before I can enjoy my homecoming.'

'You may depend on me, dear lord,' replied the old woman. 'You must surely remember how of old I was ever to be trusted. I will keep silence and help you in any way an aged woman can.'

He smiled at her, and trembling, she rose and went to fetch more water, for every drop had been spilt. But Penelope had noticed nothing of all that had passed, for she had been staring into the fire, wondering how best to order her future.

When Odysseus came to her to bid her good night, she asked him, saying, 'One thing further would I beg of you, good stranger, that you might interpret for me a dream which I had the other night. Twenty grey geese have I in the courtyard, and often do I go myself to give them grain, for they come to me when I call them and they are a pretty sight to see when they eat together from the trough. In my dream I saw the geese here, in this very hall, pecking up their corn, but a great eagle flew down from the hills and fell upon them and killed them, all the twenty, and they lay dead upon the floor. Then the eagle rose up into the sky and flew higher and higher, and the sun shone brightly upon his wings. But in my dream I wept, for my geese were slain. Yet even as I wept, the eagle came back again and alighted on the house-roof and spoke to me.

'"Weep not, Penelope," he said, "for I am your husband Odysseus, and the geese were your wooers. And when I come again to you, it shall be as a man, and as a man shall I slay the suitors, every one. For this is no dream, but reality."

'Upon that I awoke and it was dawn, and when I went to the courtyard, there were my geese, feeding on their grain, just as they had ever done. Tell me, stranger, if you can, what means this dream.'

'Surely, good queen, there can be no other meaning to it than the very one which seems most apparent, that Odysseus himself will soon be home and wreak great vengeance on your suitors.'

Penelope sighed. 'I wish I dared believe you, but truly dreams are curious things, often meaning just the contrary of what they appear to signify. But now no longer can I put off the day when I must decide my fate and leave this house which has been my home for twenty years, however loath I may be to go. Stranger, tell me if you think this well that I have thought to do. In the happy days when he lived in this his home, my husband, who was skilled in all manner of games and contests, had a favourite sport. He would set up here in the hall a row of axes crossed, and through the gaps made by the handles and the heads, he would shoot arrows, never missing; a truly clever feat. I have it in my mind to bring out my husband's bow and set up once more those axes, and bid the suitors shoot through them when they have strung the great bow. And the man who can accomplish this test of skill, him will I marry and to his home will I go, for of all the wooers he will be nearest to my husband. What think you of my plan, stranger?'

Odysseus smiled. 'It is a clever scheme that you have thought of, Queen Penelope, and I counsel you to tell your wooers of this contest soon, and to put them to the trial. But I am certain that Odysseus will be home before any among the suitors has even strung the bow, and most certainly before any one of them has shot an arrow through the axes, for it sounds a hard exploit indeed.'

Penelope rose. 'I thank you, stranger, for your kindly

words and the advice and comfort you have given me. Now do I bid you good night and pleasant rest.' She beckoned to her maids and turned and went from the hall, followed by all the women; and Odysseus was left alone.

He went to the bed which had been prepared for him in the vestibule, but he lay long awake, pondering the deeds of the morrow and planning the slaying of the suitors, before at last he fell asleep.

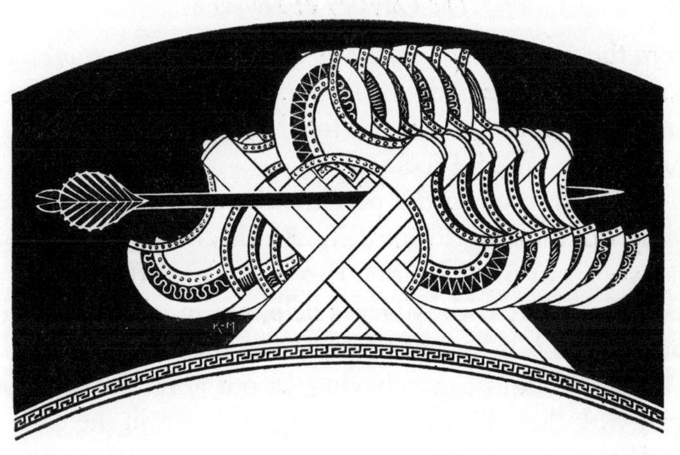

XIX

The Great Bow

THE next day was a holiday in honour of the god Apollo, patron of art and learning, and the servants in Odysseus' house were stirring early to make all things ready for an even more splendid day of feasting for the suitors than was usual.

Eurycleia bustled round the hall seeing that no one was idle, but that all were working hard in preparation for the banquet. Twelve women were set to grind the corn and barley into flour, that fresh loaves might be baked; while others polished the seats and tables in the great hall and washed the wine-bowls and the drinking-cups and the gold and silver platters; and others spread with clean draperies and fleecy rugs the chairs and stools, and strewed fresh rushes on the floor. Yet others were kept busy going to and from the well, drawing pails of water, that there might be as much as was needed when the suitors came. In the courtyard the men chopped wood for the fires; and everywhere there was work and activity.

Odysseus stood in the porch and watched all that was going on, thinking to himself, 'All this is being done for the wooers of my wife, that they may enjoy the feast-day at my cost. But with Athene's help, not much longer will they live to waste more of my substance.'

Soon Eumaeus came, having set out at dawn from the farm with three fat swine. Leaving his beasts in the courtyard he went straight to Odysseus and greeted him warmly, saying, 'Good morning to you, my friend. Tell me, how fared you at the hands of the suitors after I was gone last evening? Did their evil conduct mend?'

'They were as arrogant and as insolent as men could be,' replied Odysseus. 'Truly, they are wicked, and I only pray that the gods may bring them soon to a day of reckoning.'

As they were talking together, Melanthius the goatherd drove a flock of goats through the gate. He saw Odysseus and Eumaeus at once, and going to them said, 'So your friend is still with us, swineherd, and you are wasting your time listening to him babbling about his better days, when he had a house and servants of his own.' He laughed mockingly, and turned to Odysseus. 'You old liar, why do you not go to another house and trouble some other men, and leave the noble suitors in peace? Sooner or later I can see that I shall have to drive you away from here, and I warn you that when I take a hand in this matter, it will be long before you dare to come here again.' And with that he left them, going on into the house.

At this moment there arrived in the courtyard Philoetius, the chief of Odysseus' cowherds, who kept his cattle on the mainland where Odysseus owned some pasture-land and a farm. Philoetius had an ox and some fat goats for the suitors' feast, having brought them over to Ithaca on the ferry. He came straight to the swineherd who was an old friend of his, waving his staff in greeting. Seeing Odysseus, he smiled at him, and offering his hand, said, 'I have not seen you here before, welcome to our master's house, old stranger. I wish the good king were here himself to give you entertainment, for he was a man who would never turn away a poor wanderer. But in his absence it is his servants who must honour a guest, since the unrighteous men who despoil his house spare no word of welcome for one who has naught to offer them, and the young master and our good mistress, the queen, can have no heart, these days, for anything but grieving, may the gods protect them both.'

'Truly, may the immortal gods protect them,' echoed Eumaeus.

'When I look at you, stranger,' went on the cowherd, 'I feel a great fear that, even like you, our good king may be wandering through the world, begging his bread from unfriendly men. But even that, I suppose, would be better than that he should be dead, never to return. For while he lives there must always be hope in his heart that one day he will see Ithaca again. He was a good master to me, and he believed in my worth, for I was only a youth when he put me in charge of all his cattle on the mainland. He said that he knew that I would work for him so long as I had breath and that I could ever be trusted. And indeed, though he is far away and cannot see his words come true, I have never betrayed his trust, nor ever shall, but always will I serve him faithfully. Sometimes I long to leave this place and flee away, for I cannot bear to see the suitors of the queen wasting all my master's goods and eating the cattle that I have reared for him, increasing their number manyfold in twenty years. But for his sake, for good King Odysseus' sake, I will remain here, however hard my lot may be.'

Odysseus saw at once that here was a man who would fight for him if need be, and remembered with satisfaction the day when he had set him over his herds because he had foreseen his worth, though he had been but a lad. He said, 'Good herdsman, I can promise you that Odysseus will soon be home. He is not dead, and I tell you that before you leave the island to return to your farm, he will be here to take vengeance on the suitors.'

'If that should truly come to pass,' said Philoetius eagerly, 'then will King Odysseus see how I can fight for him. I ask no more than to strike a blow for him and for his family against these insolent thieves who have entered his home to rob it while he is far away.'

Meanwhile, the suitors were gathering at Odysseus' house, coming through the great gates in laughing, chattering groups, and crossing the courtyard to the hall where the midday meal was almost ready. Odysseus and Eumaeus and the cowherd went into the hall together, and Telemachus came forward at once and placed a chair for his father beside the big door, whispering to him, 'It is best that you sit again by the doorway, father, lest later any of them should try to escape.'

While Odysseus whispered back, 'That was well thought of, my son. It is the very place I would have chosen.'

Aloud, Telemachus said, 'You may sit there, stranger, and eat and drink your fill, and you may rely on me to protect you from any insults that may be offered to you in my own house by the men who choose to gather here.' And turning to the suitors as they were sitting down to their meal, he said, 'All you wooers of my mother, I bid you respect my guest and my house and keep from quarrelling and violence while you are in it.'

The suitors were surprised at the unaccustomed authority in Telemachus' voice and they looked at one another and shrugged their shoulders, murmuring. But of them all, only Antinous spoke out. With a sneer he addressed his companions loudly. 'I suppose we must bear with this insulting attitude of our good queen's son, or earn her displeasure.' In a lower voice he added, 'It is a pity that our plans went awry, or we should for ever have been spared the sound of that carping voice.'

Most of the suitors ignored Odysseus, where he sat beside the door, but a certain Ctesippus, a noble of great wealth, who came from the neighbouring island of Same, and was ever a man who loved to be considered quick to make a jest and to give to his companions a witty word to laugh at, now sought to amuse the other wooers at Odysseus' expense. 'My friends,' he called out, 'the ragged stranger has already been given a good meal, as is, of course, only right and seemly. But watch, for now I am going to give him an extra portion, such as is fit for the most honoured guest of all, one whose presence graces the house even of a king.' And with that he picked up a large bone from the dish before him, and flung it at Odysseus. But Odysseus moved his head quickly, and the bone struck the wall beside him.

Telemachus jumped up at once. 'If you had had the misfortune to aim better and hit your mark, Ctesippus, it would have gone ill with you, for I should have thrust my spear through your heart, and it would have been a burial and not a wedding that your parents would have celebrated for you. Listen, all you suitors of my mother,' he went on. 'I am not a child and I will not bear with this brawling and this misconduct in my house. I have yet found no way to drive you forth, so unwillingly must I bear with your presence and your feasting off my father's food and wine, but I will not stand by and see my guests insulted and provoked. If only when you have caused my death, will you be satisfied, then it is almost a better thing that you should murder me, than that I should have to see your cowardly attacks on an old man who has sought my hospitality.'

For a while they were silent, pondering his words, then one of them said, 'You have spoken well, Telemachus, and I assure you that there shall be no more mistreatment of the stranger or your slaves. But now, Telemachus, let me ask a favour of you in return. So long as you and your gracious mother could still hope that one day King Odysseus would come home, no one could blame the two of you for resenting our presence. But as he has not returned though ten years have passed since he set sail from Troy, there is surely now no hope for him, and your mother would do well to resign herself to accept the truth and choose another husband. Go, urge your mother to make up her mind and all your troubles will be over.'

'Never,' said Telemachus, 'never shall I seek to persuade my mother against her will. That have I sworn to you often before, and I swear it again now. My mother's choice shall be free and she shall make it when she wishes.'

But the only answer that the suitors gave him was to laugh as though he had been jesting. Then one after another they mocked him, saying, 'Poor Telemachus, how hard he tries to play the man and rule his household,' and, 'What a dutiful son, to have such a care for his mother's happiness.' And again, 'But think, my friends, of what this house will be like when good Penelope is married and gone. It will be filled with all the old beggars from the land of Greece, sitting at the door and eating good food, while Telemachus presides over their entertainment, a willing, careful host.' And they laughed until they held their sides, and drank ever more good wine.

But suddenly Theoclymenus the seer stood up in their midst. His face was pale and he cried out in a strange voice, 'You fools that laugh at your own destruction. I can see blood upon the floor, and the bodies of the slain; and the spirits of dead men thronging in the porch. Take heed, you suitors of the queen, before it is too late.'

But they met his words with laughter and jeering, and Eurymachus said, 'Truly, the stranger that has come from over the sea must be out of his mind. Make haste, some of you, and hurry him forth to find a welcome elsewhere, since he finds this fine house so dismal.'

'I need no one of you to help me on my way,' said Theoclymenus. 'I have two feet which will carry me from here speedily enough, for I see a terrible doom about to come on you, and not one of you shall escape it.' And flinging his cloak about him, fearfully he hastened from the house, and running down the roadway to the town, he returned to the home of Peiraeus.

And in their mirth the suitors mocked Telemachus further, 'Truly, poor youth, how unfortunate you are in your choice of guests. First is it that greedy old man who does naught but eat and drink, and now it is a mad prophet, seeing visions. Poor Telemachus, you have our sympathy. But never despair, for in time, when you are older, you will have learnt how better to pick your friends.'

It was then that it came to the mind of Penelope to try her wooers with Odysseus' bow, even as she had told her husband, thinking him to be a stranger, the night before. So calling to her Eurycleia, who kept the key of the store-room, with her and two other maids she came down from her apartments and passed through the hall to the door in the wide wall to fetch Odysseus' bow from the armoury.

Penelope herself reached up to the peg where hung the great bow, and lifted it down. It was a massive weapon fashioned of wood upon which strips of horn had been laid along the inside, while on the outer edge it was protected by a casing of strong ox-hide. It was covered with a leather sheath to protect it from the dust and damp, and as soon as Penelope had taken it out from the sheath, and seen once more the bow that her husband had so often handled, she sat down upon a stool, holding it in her arms and weeping piteously.

But after a time she rose and dried her tears, and speaking to her women, bade one of them fetch her the quiver full of arrows which lay upon a shelf, and told the other to carry the twelve double-headed axes that Odysseus had used for his sport. Then, herself bearing the bow and the quiver, she returned along the passage-way to the hall, and passing through the side door, she stood in the midst of the suitors by a pillar, and spoke to them.

'Hear me, my suitors,' she said, and they all kept silent to listen to her. 'For long enough have you feasted here with no one to prevent you, giving as the reason for your conduct your desire to win me for a wife. Therefore I have at last decided that the time has come for me to save for my son what still remains to him of his inheritance after you have wasted his possessions for more than three long years. Here in my hands I hold the bow of my dear husband Odysseus, with which he was wont to make great sport. A favourite feat of his was to shoot arrows through the space between twelve axes set up in two rows, a task not easy to accomplish. My suitors, I challenge you to prove yourselves as good men as my dear lord Odysseus, by stringing his bow and shooting through the axes, even as he so often did. Yet it is no easy feat, so there will be many who will fail to achieve it. But the man who proves himself the ablest at it, and therefore most like my lord, him will I marry and to his home will I go, quitting the house of Odysseus for ever, though my heart will ache to leave it, and for it shall I ever pine, seeing it and weeping for it even in my dreams. But come, my suitors, take up the challenge, for here before you stands the prize.' And turning to Eumaeus she bade him carry the bow and arrows to the wooers. But in her heart she hoped that all of them might fail in the trial, so that she might stay a little longer in Odysseus' house.

Like his mistress, the good swineherd wept when he

touched the bow, remembering his master and the good old days; and Antinous marked the tears and cried out with scorn, 'Look how the slave wails for his master. Cease your tears, you fool. Would you distress your mistress more? Come, give us the bow and let us try our skill with it. But I think it will not be an easy feat even to string it, such a mighty weapon it is. I remember once, in this very hall, when I was but a child, seeing Odysseus shoot through the axes, and I marvelled at his achievement.' So spoke Antinous, not belittling the difficulty of the test the suitors had been set, for he wished thus to excuse his failure should he be unable to string the bow, and to magnify his prowess should he be successful, as he secretly hoped he might.

Telemachus, his heart beating very fast, for he saw that the moment was approaching when he and his father would stand alone against their enemies, rose, and called out with a gaiety he did not feel, 'Come, lords of our land and the neighbouring isles, you are offered the hand of the fairest lady in all Ithaca. Do not hold back from the test. Let me set up the axes for you, so you may all take your turn in shooting, and may it be the best man among her suitors who wins my dear mother.'

So he set up the axes and fixed them firmly in two rows, an axe leaning alternately to the left and to the right, so that their handles crossed and the sides that were innermost of their two-headed blades were overlapping. It was through the small space between the upper part of the hafts, where they crossed, and the lower edge of the blades, that the arrow had to pass.

When the axes were arranged to his satisfaction, Telemachus said, 'Eumaeus, give me the bow, I have a mind to try myself, to see whether I am as good a man as my honoured father was. My friends the suitors will not grudge me the delay.'

He took the bow, and with all his strength tried to bend it so that it might be strung. But the tough wood and horn proved too much for him; and after the fourth attempt he laid the bow down, sighing, 'It seems that I am still too young to try such a feat, or perhaps it is that I am a poor weakling who will never equal my father in skill and strength. But it is as the gods will it, so come, my friends, take your turns and show what you can do, for you are older and better men than I.'

Antinous at once took charge, suggesting that they should, one after another, try to string the bow and shoot a single arrow through the axes, starting with the man who sat to the left of the company, and working round to the right. To this the other suitors agreed, and instantly the man who was on the extreme left strode from his place and came forward to try his luck. But though he put forth all his might, he could not string the bow.

'My friends,' he said to his companions, 'never will this bow yield to my hands, so let the next man take his turn. But I foresee that it will bring great grief to many of us here, before the day is over. Many of us there shall be who will have to woo another lady, for Penelope will never be ours.' He put down the bow and returned to his place.

Antinous was angered by his words, for he feared that the bow might be even harder to string than he had expected, and he was afraid of his own failure. 'You speak nonsense,' he said, 'and all because you have too little strength to string the bow yourself. Why should it bring great grief to us? You were ever a weakling, and there was no hope of your success. But only watch the rest of us. I warrant there will be many of us to do the deed.' He called to the goatherd, 'Come, Melanthius, fetch a brazier and some wax, that we may grease the bow to make it more pliable, and thus shall we succeed in stringing it.'

So they greased the bow with the melted wax, and one by one they tried to string it, but one by one they failed. And while they were still trying to bend the bow, Eumaeus and the cowherd went from the house and walked in the yard, talking together of their lost master, and debating on the wooers' chances to win the queen.

Odysseus, who had seen them go, slipped out after them, and calling them to him, said in a low voice, 'My friends, if Odysseus were to come home now, quite suddenly, and the suitors were to take up arms against him in his own house, for whom would you fight, for him or for them? Or would you save yourselves from both, and run away?'

'Not I,' said Philoetius. 'I would find a weapon, any one would do, and stand beside my master until I was struck down.'

'And I too,' said Eumaeus. 'I would fight for my good master's rights, and if it pleased the immortal gods that I should die, why then I should have met a good death, fighting for our king.'

Well pleased by their words, Odysseus made himself known to them, saying, 'Good herdsmen of mine, I am Odysseus, returned to his home. Soon shall I give you a chance to prove your words, and I think you will not fail me, for you are loyal men both. If you should doubt me, know me by this scar upon my leg—you both have seen it before—where I was gored by a boar's sharp tusk one day when I was hunting. You are the elder, Eumaeus, you will remember the day.'

Great was the joy with which the two faithful servants welcomed their master home, and high was their hope of seeing things in his house ordered well once more.

'We must not tarry longer here in the courtyard,' warned Odysseus, 'for our absence may be noticed and the suitors grow suspicious. Let us return to the hall, but not together. I shall go in first, and after me, singly, you must come, and this is what you must do. Eumaeus, I am going to ask the suitors to let me try my skill with the bow. If they should refuse me, you must yet bring it to me; and then, once it is safely in my hands, go quickly and tell old Eurycleia to lock and keep fast the door at the end of the hall which leads to the women's quarters, for I want none of them to enter the hall until our task is over. And you, Philoetius, are to fasten and bolt the great gates of the courtyard, so that no one can go out or come in.'

With that Odysseus returned to the hall and sat down on his stool by the door. He was soon followed by Eumaeus; and after he had closed the gates, Philoetius too came in.

It was by now the turn of Eurymachus to string the bow, all the other suitors save Antinous and himself having failed, and only the two of them remained to try. But like all those before him, Eurymachus failed too. 'What puny men this proves us,' he said bitterly, 'that we cannot do a thing which Odysseus often did. We shall be forever dishonoured in that we fell short.' And he handed the bow to Antinous.

Now, Antinous was afraid that where his companions had not succeeded he, too, would fail, so he said, 'Today is a festival in honour of immortal Apollo, and no fit day for contests of this sort. Let us put off this trial till tomorrow, when we can all try our strength once again. Leave the axes where they are to await us in the morning, and let us be merry now, and drink. Come, Medon, send the cupbearers about their tasks.'

Odysseus then spoke up. 'My noble lords,' he said, 'now that you have deferred this contest till tomorrow, I have a favour I would ask of you. I was once, when I was younger, no mean bowman, and I would like, for the sake of the time when I was youthful and active, to see whether my misfortunes have taken all my strength and weakened these arms that once were strong. Good Lord Antinous, and you, noble Eurymachus, grant me your permission to try to string the bow.'

They were angered at his request, for although it seemed to them most unlikely that an old man should succeed where a hundred young men had failed, they wanted to take no risks of being proved less skilled than a wandering beggarman; and Antinous called out furiously, 'Are you still here to molest us? Because we let you share our food and listen to our talking, do you think we shall allow you to take part in all our deeds? You have drunk too much wine and grown impertinent. Be silent, or else leave the house.'

But indignantly Penelope spoke up. 'Shame on you, Antinous, to be so discourteous to a stranger. He is the guest of myself and my son, therefore it is for us and not for you, to deny him what he wishes, if we would. But I say that he should take his turn with the rest of you, if he wants to. And should he string the bow, surely you have no fear that he would set himself up as a suitor and compete with you for my hand? Is it that of which you are afraid, Antinous and the rest of you?'

It was Eurymachus who answered her. 'Gracious queen,' he said, 'it is not that we fear that this old stranger might try to win you for his wife, it is that, should he string the bow after we have failed, all Ithaca will say of us that we are feeble and weakly and unworthy of our noble names, and so should we be disgraced.'

Penelope's eyes flashed angrily. 'No one who lives on another man's goods, shamelessly preying on his substance, can be disgraced any further than he is by his own actions, Eurymachus. Let the stranger do as he wishes. I promise that if he should succeed and string my husband's great bow, I will give him fine new clothes to travel in, and a sharp sword and a javelin to protect him on his wanderings.'

It was then that Telemachus saw that soon the battle would begin, and he thought, 'I must send my mother away to safety, for there are sights no woman should look upon.' So he said to her, 'Good mother, the bow belonged to my father, and since that is so, there is no one more fitted than I to decide who shall touch it and who shall not. It is my right to give it to whom I please, that he may try to string it or that he may take it for a gift, just as I allow. So, dearest mother, leave this matter to my authority and go to your own rooms and attend to your spinning and weaving, for the handling of bows is the care of men, not women.'

Wondering at his words, Penelope rose, and beckoning her maids and Eurycleia to follow her, she left the hall. As the old woman went, Telemachus whispered to her, 'Give me the key of the store-room, nurse, I may have need of it tonight,' and she took it from her girdle and gave it to him without a word.

As soon as the women had gone, Eumaeus took the bow and the quiver and made to carry them to Odysseus, and the suitors all cried out to forbid him, and for a moment he faltered. But Telemachus called to him in encouragement, and he went forward boldly and placed the great bow in his master's hands. Then quickly he went to the door of the women's quarters through which Penelope had just passed, and calling back the old nurse, bade her lock it and keep it locked until they should summon her to open it. Eurycleia understood at once what was about to happen, and with fear in her heart for her beloved master, she closed the door with trembling hands and made it fast. Eumaeus himself then locked the side-door leading to the store-room, and at the same time Philoetius went from the hall, and as an extra precaution, fastened the doors of the house which opened into the courtyard. Then both he and the swineherd stood near their master on the threshold of the great hall.

Meanwhile, Odysseus was looking carefully at his bow, turning it this way and that to see if in ten years it had decayed at all. But he was satisfied with what he saw. The suitors watched him and jeered, 'He thinks himself an accomplished bowman. See how he looks at it. Perchance he is a dealer in bows, or perchance he hopes to be one on the knowledge he acquires tonight.'

Calmly, without rising from the stool where he was sitting, Odysseus bent the bow and strung it, and with his

thumb he sounded the string, so that it hummed clear throughout the hall, and the suitors were amazed. He took one arrow from the quiver and fitted it to the bow, and still sitting, he took aim, and the arrow sped through the axes and lodged at the far end of the hall in the wood of the door that led to the women's quarters and the rest of the house.

Odysseus smiled, and called out to his son, 'Telemachus, the stranger to whom you showed favour and kindness has not shamed you. It seems the years have not destroyed my strength and skill. But now is the time for more feasting. Come, let the banquet begin.' And he signed to Telemachus who took up his sword and his spear and went to his father's side, before the door of the great hall.

XX

The Battle with the Suitors

ODYSSEUS rose, and taking up the quiver full of arrows, stood on the wide threshold of the door, and looked down the hall upon the suitors.

'The old man is indeed skilled and can shoot straight,' they said to one another. 'But come, let us drink and forget that our marksmanship has been put to shame by a tattered old beggar.'

'Well spoken, my fellow wooers,' said Antinous. 'Good wine was ever the best friend of man.' And he stretched forth his hand to take his cup.

Odysseus fitted a second arrow to his bow. 'I have scored one victory,' he called, 'and now is the time to aim for another mark. No one has yet hit it, but by the help of the immortal gods, my arrow shall fly home.' And with that he took careful aim at Antinous.

The young man had at that moment raised his golden cup, holding it by its two handles, and his head was tilted back to drink from it. The arrow passed right through his outstretched neck. The cup fell from his grasp and clattered to the floor, spilling the red wine; and clutching at his throat, Antinous fell dead beside it, his blood mingling with the wine upon the ground.

Instantly every suitor leapt to his feet and a great cry was raised. They all turned upon Odysseus in furious anger. 'You miserable beggarman, you have killed the peerless Antinous, the first of all the noblemen of Ithaca. You shall never leave the island alive, for with your life shall you pay for your carelessness and folly.' Thus they spoke, believing that it was by a mischance that Antinous had been killed.

But Odysseus cried out to them, 'You shameless, evil men, who have dared to woo my wife, and devour my food and use my house as though it were your own, you never thought that one day I should return and take my revenge. But, late though it may be, I have come home, and this shall be your last day upon this earth.'

'It is King Odysseus,' they said fearfully and with amazement among themselves, and some of them looked around the room for the arms that they were used to seeing there, the swords and shields upon the walls, and the spears and javelins in the stands beside the pillars. But nowhere was there a single weapon with which they might defend themselves, save only the swords which some of them wore, and the twelve axes through which Odysseus had shot his first arrow. And others looked round wildly, not for arms, but for escape; but when those who were nearest tried the two doors leading from the hall, one to the women's quarters and the other to the store-room, they found that they were locked. And Odysseus with his bow and quiver full of arrows stood before the big door leading to the vestibule.

Of all the suitors only Eurymachus found the courage to speak out. 'If you are indeed Odysseus,' he said, 'then you have reason enough to be angry at the things that have been done in your house while you were absent. But the man who was alone to blame for all these things lies dead already. Antinous, whom you have killed, it was who urged us to follow him and lay waste your property, for though the rest of us were here to woo the fair Penelope, he cared not for her. His only thought was to take your place, and be king here, in Ithaca. That is the truth, good Odysseus, the fault was his and he lies dead, so spare, I beg you, us others who remain, and we will in full restore your goods, making repayment of what we have deprived you.'

Odysseus looked at him with scorn. 'You wretched coward,' he said, 'even at the moment of your death you still speak glibly and utter lies. But it shall not save your life. No, nor the lives of any of you here, for with no other recompense shall I be satisfied, but only with your blood.'

When they heard this they knew that there was no hope for them, and trembled; but Eurymachus rallied them together. 'My friends,' he called, 'we are many and he is but one, and though he has a quiver full of arrows and his bow, we have our swords. Let us draw them and rush upon him before he has time to shoot us all.' And with that he took his sword in his hand, and giving a shout, ran at Odysseus down the hall. But long before he reached him, Odysseus had sent an arrow flying, and it struck him through the heart, and his shout faded on his lips as he sank to the floor.

A third suitor fell to a spear thrown by Telemachus, who was now left only with his sword. He whispered to Odysseus, 'I have the key of the store-room, I took it from Eurycleia. I will go and fetch us more arms, for I have no spear and the two herdsmen have no weapons, and soon your arrows will all be shot.'

'Go quickly, my son,' said Odysseus, 'while I still have arrows left, for I can hold them off so long as the arrows last.'

Taking the key of the side door from Eumaeus, Telemachus slipped down the wall of the hall, unnoticed by the suitors who were wildly trying to rush upon Odysseus, or to defend themselves from his rain of arrows by holding tables and chairs before them as if they had been shields. He reached the door and unlocked it, and leaving the hall, ran down the passage-way to the store-room. There he gathered together eight strong spears, four shields, and four helmets each crested with the flowing hair cut from a horse's tail. Burdened with these, he did not lock either door behind him, and stealing back into the hall he gave a spear and a shield and a helmet apiece to Eumaeus and Philoetius, and armed himself as well, putting up his long curls and twisting them around his head under the brazen helmet.

So long as there were arrows left in the quiver, Odysseus sent them flying down the hall, and one suitor fell to every shaft. But at last the arrows were all spent, so laying aside the bow, he put on the helmet Telemachus had brought for him, and took up two spears.

Melanthius the goatherd whispered to the suitors, 'Lords, I believe the weapons of Odysseus are kept in the store-room. We have tried the door to the passage which leads to it and found it locked. But if I could break down the door, perhaps I might find a way into the treasure chamber and bring you arms.' With that he went unobserved to the door in the side-wall, and to his surprise, found it was unlocked, for Telemachus had forgotten to fasten it. He hurried through and discovered that the door of the great store-room was also open, and went inside. Bringing out with him twelve shields and spears, he returned to the wooers, who seized upon them eagerly.

When Odysseus saw that some of the suitors had shields, he wondered at it, for he was sure that he and Telemachus had left none but two in the hall when they had cleared it of arms the evening before. And then a spear came hurtling by and lodged in the door beside him. 'Someone has been to the armoury,' he said, 'and brought out weapons for them. But surely the door is locked?'

Instantly Telemachus remembered. 'The fault is mine, father,' he said. 'I forgot to lock either of the doors.' He turned to Eumaeus. 'Go, good Eumaeus, take the keys and fasten well both doors, before they can fetch more arms.'

As he hurried away, the swineherd saw Melanthius slip through the door again, and beckoned to Philoetius to come with him; and they went together after the goatherd. They found him in the armoury, choosing out more weapons, and fell upon him and bound him with a rope they took from round a wooden chest. Then after carefully locking both the doors behind them, they returned to Odysseus' side.

Together the four of them faced the many wooers who sought to make a last effort, crying out, 'Let us all aim together at Odysseus, for with him dead, the other three will have no heart to fight on, and we may escape.'

Six among them threw each a spear, but their throws were wild, and Odysseus received not a single scratch. Then he and Telemachus and the two herdsmen flung their spears among the suitors, and to each spear there fell a man. The rest of the suitors fled to the farthest end of the hall, while Odysseus and the three others rushed forward with shouts of triumph and caught up their spears again. Once more they threw, and once more their aim was good and four men died. And among them, to the great joy of Philoetius, was Ctesippus, the man who had cast a bone at his master, killed by the cowherd's own spear.

And now panic came upon the suitors and they dropped their weapons and fled, rushing distractedly at the walls and two locked doors in their attempts to escape destruction.

'Come,' called Odysseus, 'let us fall upon them and cut them down,' and followed by Telemachus and the herdsmen, he ran along the hall, and with his sword struck down man after man, pausing for no appeals for mercy.

Holding his lyre, the minstrel Phemius stood against the wall, wondering if he had a chance to escape by the great door which was now left unguarded, and fly from thence into the courtyard. But he saw Odysseus bearing down upon him, his sword in his hand, and flinging aside his lyre, he ran forward and fell at his feet.

'Grant me mercy, King Odysseus,' he pleaded, 'for my voice is very sweet. No one in all Ithaca can sing as I. You will one day regret it if you kill me now, for all men love good singing, and a poet's life should be sacred for the sake of his art.'

'You sang for the suitors,' said Odysseus. 'I heard you myself.'

'And what if I sang for them? A singer cannot be silent so long as there are men to hear him sing. And if those men be evil, it does the song no harm, nor yet the singer, that he pleases them. And to a poet, more than the worth of those who hear them, is the value of his songs.'

The minstrel's long hair grasped in his left hand and his sword at his throat, Odysseus hesitated, looking down upon the young man's face and wondering whether to spare his life or not. But Telemachus saw him and called out to him, 'Do not kill Phemius, father, for his singing gives great joy. And spare Medon, too, for he is innocent of ill doing, and only served the suitors when they demanded it. And more, it was he who warned mother that the suitors were plotting against my life.' He looked around. 'But I fear he may be killed already, for I see him not. It grieves me that he should have died, for he often played with me and told me tales when I was a child.'

But Medon had hidden himself beneath a rug behind a great chair, where he lay crouched; and when he heard Telemachus' words, he came forth from his hiding-place and ran to him, imploring him, 'Do not let your father kill me, for I have ever wished well to you and to the queen.'

Odysseus smiled at him. 'Then go quickly to the courtyard and wait there until I have finished all I have to do in here.' His left hand unclenched and released Phemius' hair. 'And the minstrel may go with you,' he said.

Phemius delayed only long enough to snatch up his lyre

before following Medon out of the hall to the great house-door, where with trembling hands they unfastened the latch and fled into the courtyard.

One by one Odysseus hunted down the suitors, until none remained alive; then he spoke to Telemachus, saying, 'Go, my son, and call Eurycleia.'

Telemachus knocked on the door at the far end of the hall and shouted to the old nurse until she came and unlocked it to him, then he led her to Odysseus. When she saw her master standing amid his slain enemies, she raised a cry of victory, but Odysseus silenced her. 'It is not seemly to rejoice over the dead,' he said. 'Restrain your triumph and let your joy be silent. But I would have you tell me which of all my servants have been faithful to me, and which of them have served too well the suitors.'

'There are but twelve of all your slaves, and Melanthius the goatherd,' she replied, 'who have grown out of hand and disobedient, preferring to follow the demands of the suitors than to obey the queen.'

'Send the twelve to me,' ordered Odysseus.

When the disloyal servants came, he set them to carry the slain suitors from the hall and lay them outside the house, and to sweep and clean the hall and put the furniture to rights. Then, their last task done, he sent them into the courtyard, and there the two herdsmen killed them. And with them died Melanthius the goatherd.

Then Odysseus called to Eurycleia to bring brimstone and fire to purify the hall, and to bid Penelope and her women come down to him. But she protested, 'You will surely not meet your wife dressed still in those rags? Let me bring you clothes more fitting to your rank, dear child.'

Odysseus laughed at her. 'Hurry, good nurse, and do as I tell you, there will be time enough for fine garments later.'

So she went off to fetch sulphur and a brazier, murmuring and complaining to herself about the wilfulness of men, and how they never would grow up.

When the serving-women heard that Odysseus was home, they flocked into the hall to greet him, with tears of joy. And of all the older women, there was not one he did not recognize, calling them all by their names.

But Eurycleia went to Penelope's room and found her asleep upon her couch. 'Wake up, dear mistress, wake up,' she called eagerly. 'Our Odysseus has come home and all the suitors are dead.'

Penelope sat up and rubbed her eyes. 'The troubles in this house have crazed you. You have lost your wits, nurse, or else this is a dream.'

'It is no dream,' said the old woman. 'Odysseus is downstairs and he has slain the suitors. The stranger whom they mocked at, he is our king. To be sure, he looks many years older than one might have expected, but perils and dangers and misfortunes age a man like nothing else. I knew my master's voice as soon as I heard it, and then I saw the scar upon his leg where he was wounded by a boar. Get up, mistress, and come and greet your husband.'

Penelope jumped from her bed happily and kissed Eurycleia. Then she grew solemn again. 'Oh nurse,' she said, 'your tidings are too good, and I dare not believe them. Surely it is one of the immortal gods in the shape of the old stranger who has done this thing, and not my dear husband. For it is certain by this time that he must have perished far away.'

'How wary you are, my child,' laughed the old nurse. 'Come with me and I will show you Odysseus.'

So, her mind filled with a great turmoil of joy and hope and fear, Penelope went down to the hall. There she saw Odysseus sitting by one of the pillars near the fire. She hesitated in the doorway, wondering whether she should go to him and call him husband and embrace him, or whether she should question him further to find if it were really he. She watched him for a few moments undecided, and then she thought that surely her Odysseus could not have grown so old in only twenty years, and that the stranger must be someone else. She went slowly to a chair on the other side of the fire, and stared at him, trying to recognize him; believing at one moment that she knew his features, and then at the next thinking herself to be mistaken because he was too old.

Telemachus stood close by, surprised at his mother's strange behaviour. 'Dearest mother,' he said, 'you have hoped and prayed for twenty years that father would come home. Now he is here, you sit like a statue and have no word to say to him. Would any other wife act thus?'

'Indeed, Telemachus,' she replied, 'I do not know what to think or say or do. The suddenness of everything that has happened here today has robbed me of all action. But if the stranger really is Odysseus, I shall know him when I have questioned him.'

Many another man would have been dismayed by this cold reception, but not Odysseus. He was delighted at his wife's prudence and caution, feeling it to be almost worthy of himself. 'Go, Telemachus, and leave your mother and myself to talk together. I shall surely prove to her that I really have come home. But first let me please old Eurycleia and bathe, and dress myself as befits a king. That perhaps will help our good queen to know me.'

He went with Telemachus, leaving Penelope sitting beside the fire, still wondering and hoping. Flinging off his rags he took a bath in a huge cauldron of warm water, and as he stepped forth from the water, Athene gave him back again his own appearance. In a new tunic of white linen with a golden belt, and a purple cloak embroidered with a border of green, he returned once more to the hall. And Penelope looked up and saw him come, his own self, as he would have been after only twenty years from home. No longer the old stranger with his thin white hair and his wrinkled cheeks, but Odysseus, with his long dark hair and his bright eyes and the smile that she loved so well. But her joy was so great that she still dared not believe in it, and stayed quite quietly, watching him.

He sat beside her and laughed a little. 'How strange you are,' he said gently. 'After all these years I come home, and you are silent. I had thought that all women talked too much, but it seems that I am wrong.' Teasing her, he turned to Eurycleia, 'Come, nurse, I am tired, find me a room and make me up a bed. My wife has nothing to say to me, so I may as well go to sleep.'

Quickly Penelope looked round and spoke to the nurse. 'That is well thought of,' she said. 'If he is really my husband, he must sleep in the bed which he himself made. Move it out of my bedroom, Eurycleia, and make it up comfortably for him with warm rugs and blankets.'

'Indeed,' said Odysseus sharply, 'what has been happening to my bed? For I built that bed myself, taking as the headpost an olive-tree that grew beside the house, lopping off the branches and trimming the trunk, and fastening the frame with its webbing of leather straight to the post. Then around my bed I built the room, as a bedchamber for myself and my bride. No one could move my bed without cutting down the headpost that was once a tree.'

When she heard him speak thus, Penelope knew that he was indeed Odysseus, for he had not failed in the test that she had set him, but had known the secret of the fashioning of his bed. No longer she feared to trust her joy, and jumping up she ran to him and kissed him. 'Do not be angry, dear Odysseus, that I doubted you at first. Too many lies have been told to me, and too much ill doing have I seen in all these years to dare to rely on any man. But now at last I know that it is truly you.'

Happy and joyful in their reunion, they retired to rest, and long into the night Odysseus talked and told Penelope of all his adventures, and many were the questions that she asked him of all that he had seen. And when she had heard the story of the Cicones and the Lotus-eaters and Aeolus; and shuddered at the cruelty of Polyphemus and the Laestrygonians; when she had listened eagerly to the tale of Circe and the Sirens and Scylla and Charybdis; and shed a tear at the dread fate that had come upon his men when they had slain the cattle of the sun; when she had heard of Calypso and the raft and the kind Phaeacians; and after she had questioned him on each of them, they both fell asleep, and slept until the dawn.

XXI

Laertes

IN the morning Odysseus set out with Telemachus for his father's farm, that old Laertes might learn the good news. They walked across the hills to the wide, low farmhouse, set about with fields and orchards of apples, figs, and pears. Olive-trees too, were there in abundance, and a fine vineyard, and gardens with vegetables and herbs.

When they arrived, Telemachus went into the house, and Odysseus found Laertes working among the vines. He wore an old tunic with patches, leathern leggings and gloves and a tattered goatskin cap; and he looked more like an old slave than the father of a king.

Odysseus, who ever loved to speak unrecognized with people who were familiar to him and see what they would say, greeted his father as a stranger, saying, 'Who are you, old man, that your gardens are so well cared for, while you yourself are so ill clad? Are you a slave whose master neglects him? Truly, your industry deserves better treatment than this. But somehow I think that you are not a slave, for there is yet a nobility about you, in spite of your clothes, and you look to me like a great man who has fallen on evil times.'

Old Laertes looked up with a sigh. 'Stranger,' he said, 'for you must be a stranger or you would not need to ask all this, you have come to Ithaca at an unhappy time. A fine welcome would my son Odysseus have given you, and royally would he have entertained you, as was his way, had he been home. But, alas, I fear he must be dead. Yet tell me, stranger, who you are and whence you come.'

'I come from Alybas,' replied Odysseus, wondering what his father would say in reply, 'and there I once met Odysseus, your son.'

At his words the old man wept, and quickly Odysseus sought to spare him further grief. 'Dear father,' he said, 'I am your son. I have come home at last, and all the suitors are slain in my house.'

But the old man shook his head. 'Too many griefs have come upon me,' he said sadly. 'Such great joy could not be true. If you are indeed my son, then prove it to me.'

Odysseus thought a moment, then he said, 'See this scar upon my leg, where once a boar gored me. You will remember it. But if that is not enough, then will I tell you something else. One day when I was a boy I walked with you in the orchard here and asked you to give to me all the trees I liked best, and you said they should be mine.

Thirteen pear-trees were they, ten apples, and forty figs. And as well you gave to me fifty rows of vines. Do you remember that?'

At this old Laertes flung his arms around Odysseus' neck and embraced his son whom he had thought never to see again. And for a while their joy was too great for them to think of other things. Then Laertes said, 'But tell me, my son, did you say that you had slain the suitors?'

'Every one of them, father.'

'Then, my son, all the noblemen of Ithaca and the lords from the neighbouring isles will be against us. What will you do to save yourself?'

'I am their king,' said Odysseus, 'and the suitors were evil men. In the end all must be well for us. But let us go to the house now, and eat and discuss our plans, how we shall act should the townspeople rise in anger.'

At the farm a feast had been prepared on the orders of Telemachus, to celebrate the return of Odysseus, who was joyously welcomed by the servants as they came in from the fields. And together, with great gladness, they sat down to enjoy the good food spread out before them. And Laertes put away his rags and wore once again clothes worthy of his rank. 'I wish I had been with you yesterday, my son,' he said wistfully, when they told him of the battle in the hall. 'Then would you have all seen that I am not so old that I cannot strike a blow for the right.'

In the assembly place the men of Ithaca gathered to discuss the return of their king and the slaying of the suitors in Odysseus' house. The first to speak was Eupeithes, the father of Antinous, he who had once joined the Taphian pirates and been condemned by his countrymen for his deeds. 'This is indeed a grievous crime,' he said, 'and it must be avenged. Odysseus is our enemy, and he must die.'

But Medon the herald stood up and said, 'I was in the house of Odysseus myself when the wooers were slain, and I swear that there must have been a god with him, else could not four men alone have slain more than a hundred.'

Old Lord Halitherses now spoke. 'Good men of Ithaca,' he said, 'all this that has happened was the suitors' fault. Had they been less wild in their ways and listened more to reason, then would they be alive today. It is not Odysseus who is to blame for their deaths, but they themselves. This do I truly believe.'

One half of the townsmen agreed with his words, but the others sided with Eupeithes. They ran to their homes and gathered up their weapons, and with him at their head, set off for Laertes' farm, where they had heard Odysseus to be.

Odysseus and his family saw them in the distance, coming over the hills, and armed themselves to meet them, making ready to fight if need should be.

But from far-off Mount Olympus, great Zeus, father of gods and men, looked down on little Ithaca and called to Athene, saying, 'Now should you be satisfied, my daughter, now Odysseus is safely home and his enemies are slain. But it is not our will that there should be more bloodshed in Ithaca, so go yourself and see that all is settled peaceably, and Odysseus restored to his power as a king.'

Willingly Athene left Olympus to obey him, and going to where Odysseus, with his father and his son and their faithful servants, waited, armed and ready, for Eupeithes and his friends, she filled with strength and courage old Laertes, and he grasped his spear firmly and poised it; and when the attackers came within a throwing distance, he flung the spear and killed Eupeithes. And there were very few to regret the father of Antinous, for he had ever been disliked in Ithaca.

Then Zeus sent a flash of lightning, and Athene called in a mighty voice that all fighting was to cease; and instantly, in terror, Eupeithes' followers fled.

And no one again questioned Odysseus' right to avenge himself upon the wicked suitors, and from that time he was once more paid every honour as king of Ithaca. And all his days he dwelt in peace with his dear wife, Penelope, happy and prosperous and well beloved, in his own home, as Teiresias had prophesied he should.

PRINTED IN GREAT BRITAIN
AT THE UNIVERSITY PRESS, OXFORD
BY VIVIAN RIDLER
PRINTER TO THE UNIVERSITY

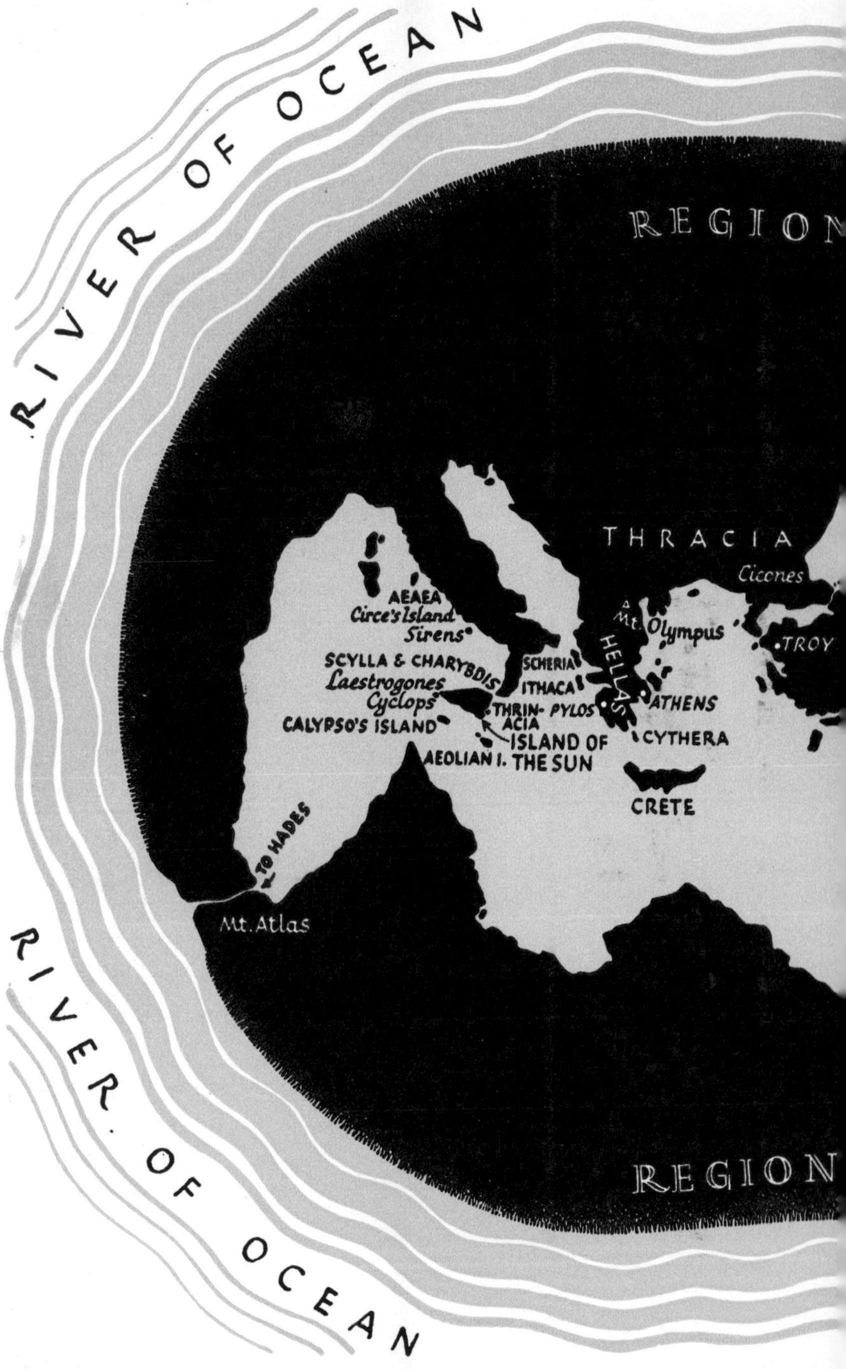

RIVER OF OCEAN

REGION

THRACIA
Cicones
Mt. Olympus
TROY
HELLAS
AEAEA
Circe's Island
Sirens
SCYLLA & CHARYBDIS
Laestrogones
Cyclops
CALYPSO'S ISLAND
SCHERIA
ITHACA
THRIN-ACIA
PYLOS
ATHENS
ISLAND OF THE SUN
AEOLIAN I.
CYTHERA
CRETE
TO HADES
Mt. Atlas

REGION

RIVER OF OCEAN